The L‑

PIERRE MARTORY was born in Bay⌐ ⌐ grew up in M⌐ ⌐rco and joined North Africa's F⌐ ⌐ring the Second W⌐ War. He published the novel *Phéb⌐* ⌐riage with Denoël in 1⌐ ⌐d worked as drama and music critic ⌐s-Match for over twenty yea⌐ ⌐ March 1956, Martory met John Ashbery, then on a Fulbright Scholarship in Paris, where they lived together for nine years. In 1962, Ashbery dedicated his poetry collection *The Tennis Court Oath* to Martory. In the 197⌐⌐ Martory collaborated with the artist Francis Wishart on a volume of text and etchings entitled *Le Père-Lachaise*. Ashbery translated Martory's first poetry collection, *Every Question but One*, in 1990 and in 1994 Sheep Meadow P⌐⌐ in the United States published Martory's first full-length volume of ⌐ry, *The Landscape Is behind the Door*. A collection of poems in French, ⌐⌐eur de jours (Sheep Meadow Press–Alyscamps Press), appeared in 1997. ⌐⌐ory died in Paris on 5 October 1998. Most recently, Artery Editions ⌐⌐lished *Oh, lac / Oh, Lake*, a bilingual edition of twenty Martory poems, ⌐⌐slated by John Ashbery, with artwork by Francis Wishart.

⌐N ASHBERY was born in Rochester, New York, in 1927. He has ⌐l'shed more than twenty collections of poetry, beginning in 1953 with ⌐⌐lot and Other Poems. In 1976, *Self-Portrait in a Convex Mirror* won the ⌐⌐zer, National Book Award, and National Book Critics Circle Award. ⌐ latest book of poems is *A Worldly Country*, published by Carcanet in ⌐. His art writings are collected in *Reported Sightings: Art Chronicles 1957–* ⌐ (Carcanet, 1990) and his literary essays appear in the Charles Eliot ⌐⌐n Lectures, *Other Traditions* (Harvard University Press, 2000), and in ⌐*d Prose* (Carcanet, 2004). Widely honoured internationally, he is the ⌐⌐nt of the Robert Frost Medal from the Poetry Society of America, the ⌐⌐e Stevens Award from the Academy of American Poets, the Gold ⌐ for Poetry from the American Academy of Arts and Letters, the ⌐ Bienek Prize for Poetry from the Bavarian Academy of Fine Arts ⌐ch), the Antonio Feltrinelli International Prize for Poetry from the ⌐emia Nazionale dei Lincei (Rome), and the Grand Prix de Biennales ⌐ationales de Poésie (Brussels), all given for lifetime achievement. His *Notes from the Air: Selected Later Poems* won the 2008 Griffin International Poetry Prize (Toronto). In 2002 he was named Officier of the Légion d'Honneur of the Republic of France.

Books by John Ashbery from Carcanet Press

Poetry
A Wave
A Worldly Country
And the Stars Were Shining
April Galleons
As We Know
Can You Hear, Bird
Chinese Whispers
Flow Chart
Girls on the Run
Hotel Lautréamont
The Mooring of Starting Out
Selected Poems
Self-Portrait in a Convex Mirror
Shadow Train
Wakefulness
Your Name Here

Fiction
A Nest of Ninnies (with James Schuyler)

Plays
Three Plays

Criticism and Essays
Reported Sightings: Art Chronicles 1957–1987
Selected Prose (edited by Eugene Richie)

PIERRE MARTORY

The Landscapist

Selected Poems

Translated with an introduction by
JOHN ASHBERY

Edited by
ROSANNE WASSERMAN
and
EUGENE RICHIE

CARCANET

First published in Great Britain in 2008 by
Carcanet Press Limited
Alliance House
Cross Street
Manchester M2 7AQ

First published in the United States of America in 2008 by the
Sheep Meadow Press, PO Box 1345, Riverdale, NY 10471, USA

Copyright © 1961, 1967, 1990, 1994, 1996, 1997, 2000, 2001, 2008
    by The Estate of Pierre Martory
English translation copyright © 1961, 1989, 1990, 1991, 1992, 1993,
    1994, 1995, 1996, 2000, 2001, 2002, 2008 by John Ashbery
Introduction copyright © 2008 by John Ashbery
Photograph of Pierre Martory © 2008 by John Ashbery
Photograph of Pierre Martory and John Ashbery © 1994, 2008 by
    John Ashbery

A CIP catalogue record for this book is available from
the British Library
ISBN 978 1 84777 000 4

The publisher acknowledges financial assistance
from Arts Council England

Designed and typeset by the Sheep Meadow Press
Printed and bound in England by SRP Ltd, Exeter

Table of Contents

Oh, lac / Oh, Lake

Uncollected Poems

For M'Barek Mekshoun

Pierre Martory. Pierrefonds, France. August, 1956.

Introduction

John Ashbery

Pierre Martory was born on December 1, 1920, in Bayonne in southwest France, and christened Pierre-Jean Martory; he seldom used his middle name, perhaps because a brother, Jean, was born scarcely a year later. Martory is a French version of the Catalan name Martorell; there is a village of St. Martory in the French Pyrenees. His father was a career army officer; his mother, a Basque woman, died when he was two, after giving birth to Jean. He spent the first seven years of his childhood happily pampered by poor but doting aunts and grandparents, and attending a Catholic grade school.

Martory lost this warm extended family when his father returned from assignment in North Africa, remarried, and took the two boys back to Morocco with him. His father soon had other children with his new wife, and broke off all contact with the Bayonne relatives. He even falsely told his son that his grandparents were dead: Martory was delighted to find them alive and loving as ever when the family moved back to Bayonne when he was eighteen.

He spent much of his childhood in Morocco. Despite life with a stepmother and an authoritarian father who beat him and his several half-brothers and sisters often and never allowed them to have any toys, Martory was happy there. And his school career during these years was remarkable; at twelve, he wrote an essay that won first prize in all of France; Martory remembered the award ceremony, held at the Sorbonne. He was writing poetry, as well: he stated in an interview, "Whenever I had a dissertation at the *lycée*, sometimes I wrote them in verse."[1] He loved Morocco and visited there frequently in his later years.

After studies in Morocco, he entered the Ecole des Sciences Politiques (School of Political Science) in Paris in the autumn of 1939, having received his *baccalauréat* in Bayonne that spring. In June

---

[1] Interview with Rosanne Wasserman, *The American Poetry Review*, vol. 22, no. 5 (Sept./Oct. 1993), p. 12.

1940, he escaped Paris on the last train to leave the Gare d'Austerlitz before the Germans arrived. On that harrowing journey, he saw the station at Tours in flames, as the train passed through—it had been bombed by the Italian forces. After spending some time at home, he set out on foot across Vichy-controlled southern France, the unoccupied zone. Arrested and briefly imprisoned in Lyon for not having the proper papers, he eventually made his way to North Africa, joined the French Army (soon to become the Free French Army), and ended up fighting alongside the Allied forces in Tunisia. He began writing poetry seriously during those years in the army.

After the war, Martory suffered from a deep depression for which he was hospitalized for a while. He drifted through a variety of jobs before moving to Paris: he taught at the short-lived and unlikely-sounding Biarritz American University for GI's, held in what was rumored to be a former brothel, with a ceiling decorated by Matisse; later, he was an airlines clerk in Bordeaux. Back in Paris, he worked for TWA, then as assistant to the anthropologist Marcel Griaule, until the latter's death in 1956. Subsequently he became a parliamentary secretary, and in 1962, an editor at the weekly newsmagazine *Paris-Match*. There, as music and drama critic, he contributed a weekly page on the arts until his retirement in 1985.

In the post-war years, he was also part of a loose-knit group of Parisian writers that included Hubert Juin and Hervé Bazin; they would meet at a café on the Ile Saint-Louis to declaim their poems to one another. This was the only time he ever frequented a literary milieu. In 1952, he moved to Munich for a year and a half, where he studied singing informally; when he returned, the group had dispersed, and he did not resume contact with the other writers.

Meanwhile, he had published a novel—*Phébus ou le beau mariage*—a Mauriac-like tale of an embittered provincial family—with the publisher Denoël in 1953; his editor was the esteemed Robert Kanters. The book received excellent reviews and seemed to augur a successful career as a novelist for Martory. But Kanters turned down his second novel on account of its homosexual theme. In the fifties, before the arrival on the scene of Barthes, Foucault, and gay writers, homosexuality was very much taboo in intellectual circles, reflecting an antipathy even more pronounced in predominantly left-wing France than it was in McCarthy-era America. Martory then submitted a third novel to Kanters, who liked it and agreed to publish it. But when Kanters asked him to change the ending, Martory withdrew the book in a fit of pique, and never tried to publish anything else. Years later, in his memoirs, Kanters, himself a homosexual, wondered what had happened to the brilliant young author of *Phébus*, and Martory couldn't resist writing him a note reminding him that he had played a certain role in his withdrawal from the scene.

That episode ended his career as a published man of letters, except for a few poems that appeared in now-forgotten little magazines in the early 1950s and 1960s. Consequently, although he wrote countless articles on music and theater during his twenty-five years at *Paris-Match*, Martory's poetry is little known in his native France. He seldom even showed it to anyone (myself excepted) who might be interested in it. Nevertheless, he continued to write poetry and fiction almost constantly. In the 1960s, I translated some of his poetry for the English-language reviews *Locus Solus* and *Art and Literature*.

Martory pursued other arts: his study of singing in Munich developed into a hobby practiced almost daily throughout his life. Possessed of a fine tenor voice and fluent in German, he was especially fond of Mozart's operas and Schubert's lieder. He was also an authority on French and American popular songs and films, particularly of the thirties and forties. One of his most vivid memories was of attending a showing of the Ann Miller vehicle *Reveille with Beverly* while a soldier in North Africa; the audience consisted mainly of GI's and totally mystified Moroccans.

In later years, Martory led a solitary life, his main friends a young Moroccan family whose children he adored, and Denis Demonpion, then a journalist at *Match,* now an editor of *Le Point* and author of a biography of the actress Arletty as well as a study of the novelist Michel Houellebecq. Another friend was Francis Wishart, with whom Martory collaborated on a volume of text and etchings entitled *Le Père-Lachaise*—the cemetery near where he lived and where his ashes are now scattered. Martory and I visited one another often in Paris, New York City, and Hudson, New York, and also often traveled together.

Since Martory shunned literary politics and people in general (though in social situations his charm could be irresistible—the poet Ann Lauterbach once said that his charm devolved back to the original meaning of "spell"), I translated many of his poems in order to make them known at least in English. This work resulted in a chapbook, *Every Question but One* (New York: Intuflo Editions, The Groundwater Press, 1990), and a more substantial collection, *The Landscape Is behind the Door* (New York: Sheep Meadow Press, 1994). There were some good reviews, and his poetry soon began to appear in such magazines as *Poetry* (Chicago), *American Poetry Review*, and *The New Yorker*. American colleges and other poetry venues invited him to give readings, and he was particularly gratified when a poster at the Institut Français in Boston billed him as a great poet still undiscovered by the French. This situation seemed about to change: in 1997, Sheep Meadow Press published *Veilleur de jours*, a volume of his poems in French, which was to be distributed in France by Alyscamps Press, a publisher of English books in Paris. But for unexplained reasons, the distributor dropped the project, and the copies have never been put on sale in France. Most recently, Artery Editions in England published a bilingual edition of twenty of his poems, entitled *Oh, Lake/Oh, lac*, with artwork by Wishart.

I first met Pierre in March 1956, having recently arrived in France on a Fulbright scholarship. We became instant friends, and soon began living together, an arrangement that lasted nine years, until my reluctant departure from France in 1965. My book *The Tennis Court Oath* (1962) is dedicated to him. Pierre, a voracious and omnivorous reader with a preference for history, biography, and memoirs (he reread those of Saint-Simon in their mammoth entirety after an improved Pléiade edition appeared), was the ideal guide to France and things French for an American; in addition, his take on them had something distinctly and irreverently American about it.

He always had more American (and Moroccan) friends than French ones; he used to say, "I love France but I hate ze French!"

Even with Pierre's help it took me a long time to become fluent in French, and thus I began to read his poetry only after we had known each other for a year or more. I was also reading other contemporary and classical French poetry, and as I became familiar with its tropes, it began to strike me that his was quite different. He had assimilated the moderns, especially René Char, along with the classical "canon" that French students are forced to ingest, but my still relatively unschooled eye could find no resemblances, or very few, between his poetry and French poetry of the past or present.

In fact, with the exception of a few older poets such as Char and Francis Ponge, French poetry in the decade following World War II was in a period of doldrums. Something similar had happened in England, where the thirties brio of W. H. Auden, F. T. Prince, Louis MacNeice, and Nicholas Moore had been supplanted by Philip Larkin's austerity; and in America, where Delmore Schwartz, the early Randall Jarrell, and John Berryman were eclipsed by Robert Lowell and the later Auden, Berryman, and Jarrell.

French poets must struggle to escape the crystalline tyranny of the French language; even the Surrealists at their most fantastic built on its classical foundations. It must also be said that there were for decades far fewer opportunities for poets in France than in the U. S. A.; there was a mere handful of poetry reviews, controlled by rival cliques, and poetry readings were quite uncommon. Things have improved in recent years. There is a new boldness in French poetry and a new interest in experimental American poetry, as well as several lively, eclectic reviews such as the Marseilles-based *Banana-Split*, which published Martory's "Prose des Buttes-Chaumont"—his first published poem in France in more than thirty-five years.

As younger French poets have become aware of new American experiments with language, and vice versa (thanks in some degree to the cross-pollinating efforts of *américainistes* like Emmanuel Hocquard, Serge Fauchereau, and Olivier Brossard), our younger generation has begun to have an impact in France; meanwhile, a spate of recent translations has enabled English-speaking readers to assess the achievements of major figures such as Edmond Jabès and Michel Deguy, and of such innovative younger poets as Pascalle Monnier and Anne Portugal.

For me, Martory's work ranks with that of the finest contemporary French poets. As Dara Wier has said, one reads Martory's poems as if he "were at your side reading them with you: his point of view is that palpable, that intimate. . . . Sometimes it seems as if he is one of the rarest of a rare sort, one who takes everything and everyone grievously seriously—himself excepted: that is his modesty, ever present in his poems."[2]

Looking today for the antecedents of Martory's poetry, I am forced to speculate, since for some reason we rarely discussed our work with each other. The flavor of his poetry is unique, located somewhere between Paris and New York. Yet, despite his many American friends, and although he had probably seen more American films than most other Frenchmen (starting at the age of five with Lon Chaney's *Hunchback of Notre Dame*), he mistrusted America and her political institutions.

Not surprisingly, his work doesn't seem to derive from any of the various modernist (or post-modernist) French schools, though there are echoes of "fringe" surrealists like Pierre Reverdy and the chameleon-like Raymond Queneau, whose wicked, witty and wistful novels of French lowlife are the perfect antidote to existentialism and must have affected Martory's own writing. The austerity of Pierre-Jean Jouve's poetry and the cloudy fantasy of Jules Supervielle's also come to mind.

There is a touch of the gaiety of Charles Trenet and of René Clair's early films; of the melancholy of singers like Florelle and Piaf, and the song *Sombre Dimanche* ("Gloomy Sunday"), which seems to sum up the thirties. (As a child Martory and his brother were forbidden to listen to it by their stepmother, who had heard it could lead to suicide.) A poem from the early fifties, "Blues," epitomizes the childish expectancy and the jaundiced *spleen de Paris* that mingle in the best work of this extraordinary poet. Both the humor and the

[2]In *Dark Horses: Poets on Overlooked Poems*, ed. Joy Katz and Kevin Prufer (Champaign: University of Illinois, 2006).

sadness in his poems are always rendered with an unemphatic clarity like that of Mozart, his favorite composer.

His fluency in German makes me aware of trace elements of Hölderlin, Rilke, and Trakl (the latter especially in "Red and Black Lake"), though again these are only educated guesses. We both shared an enthusiasm for Raymond Roussel, whose otherworldly landscapes are perhaps "behind the door," especially in a longish poem called "Evenings in Rochefort" which I translated for *Locus Solus* in the sixties. In the end, the most fruitful comparison seems to be with Arthur Rimbaud, and not because Martory's poetry resembles his, but because both are similar in resembling no one else.

Whether Martory was influenced by American models I don't know, though when we first met he was reading Emily Dickinson, T. S. Eliot, and Gertrude Stein. He certainly hadn't read my poetry yet, though I find a curious prefiguring of it in poems of his written before we knew each other, such as "Blues" and "Ma Chandelle est morte." And after I began translating him, that is, after I began to realize that his marvelous poetry would likely remain unknown unless I translated it and brought it to the attention of American readers, I started to find echoes of his work in mine. His dreams, his pessimistic résumés of childhood that are suddenly lanced by a joke, his surreal loves, his strangely lit landscapes with their inquisitive birds and disquieting flora, have been fertile influences for me, though I hope I haven't stolen anything—well, better to steal than borrow, as Eliot more or less said.

All of which may be a way of saying that there is no very easy way to describe Martory's poetry. It is *sui generis* and it deserves to be read. And reread.

Editors' Note

The Landscapist offers all of John Ashbery's finished translations of Pierre Martory's poems, in a bilingual format with their French originals. These translations have previously appeared in periodicals, anthologies, and pamphlets, and in Martory's own book-length collections. The Landscapist is organized chronologically by book collections. Four poems published originally in the chapbook Every Question but One appeared later in somewhat different versions in The Landscape Is behind the Door. These poems are included here only in the Landscape section, since we chose to use the latest possible versions. Ashbery has made occasional emendations to poems in this volume, as well. The section entitled "Uncollected Poems" refers to translations that have never appeared before in book form. In Appendix I, "Bridge Passed" is a translation from a lost French original. "Tchat," in Appendix II, was written by Martory in both French and English. In Appendix III are two poems in which the English and French texts vary widely; the poems from which Ashbery translated were lost, but we found later versions by Martory. The book features six previously unpublished translations. For more information, please consult the bibliography in Appendix IV. We note the existence of hundreds of untranslated poems that remain in manuscript in the archives of the Ashbery Resource Center (www.flowchartfoundation.org/arc), a project of the Flow Chart Foundation for Bard College.

Portions of Ashbery's introduction have appeared previously, in Every Question but One, The Landscape Is behind the Door, and in Martory's obituary in The Guardian, London (November 18, 1998).

We would like to thank David Kermani for all he has done to facilitate this volume of Martory's poetry; Michael Ward von Üchtrup for his preliminary organization of Martory's literary archive; Micaela Morrissette, a former director of the Ashbery Resource Center, for her assistance with manuscript research; Leslie Morris, Curator of Modern Books and Manuscripts, Houghton Library, Harvard University, for her assistance with manuscript research in the Houghton Library; Dr. Katia Sainson of Towson University, who carefully edited galleys for the French versions of the poems; Olivier Brossard and Claire Guillot, for their help with manuscripts and with problems in the French and its translation; Denis Demonpion and Amy Rourke, Martory's close friends in Paris, for their assistance with obtaining manuscripts and with our Paris research work; Wai Wan Lam, for her typing and editing of the poems; Sean Garritty of Sheep Meadow Press, who both designed the book and handled the galley proofs; and Stanley Moss of Sheep Meadow Press, for his continued, enthusiastic support of Martory's work.

Pierre Martory and John Ashbery. Paris, France. 1957.

From: *Every Question but One*

Image

Un rideau léger où s'engouffre
le courant d'air du corridor
s'entrouvre
et laisse voir dans la chambre un miroir
reflétant le lit qui supporte
comme des genoux de pietà
un corps alangui sur ses rêves
n'y touche pas il est figé
mouvement chaleur et *tanti palpiti*
dans le geste d'éternité
saisi par l'oeil la main l'esprit
extérieurs à sa permanence
tel dieu ayant créé le monde
et l'ayant reconnu parfait
lui aurait imposé
pour unique futur
de demeurer semblable
à l'instant
où il fut
finit

Image

A light curtain in which the draft
from the corridor is swallowed up
opens slightly
to reveal a mirror in the bedroom
reflecting the bed which supports
like the knees in a pietà
a body languishing on its dreams
don't touch it it has stiffened
movement warmth and *tanti palpiti*
in the gesture of eternity
seized by the eye the hand the mind
exterior to its permanence
as God having created the world
would have imposed
its only future
to remain identical
to the moment
when it was
finished

Dialogue

Il dit   Je te regarde comme ma propre image
Il dit   Je suis le miroir et les deux faces du miroir

Il dit   Tu m'appartiens comme je me possède
Il dit   Je ne veux être ni à toi ni à moi

Il dit   J'entre météorite et je brûle tes forêts
Il dit   Je suis dedans lorsque je suis dehors

Il dit   Je te construis et te métamorphose
Il dit   Ce que j'ai trouvé je ne le change pas

Il dit   Que je te touche et nous ne sommes qu'un
Il dit
        Je te touche et le ciel se sépare des eaux
        Des oiseaux s'installent dans les abres
        Car ils attendaient cet instant depuis l'instant
        Où poussant la porte des jours
        Des oiseaux s'installaient dans les arbres
        Chacun trouvant sous un nuage le nuage
        Où recueillir son impatience et la briser
        Car ils attendaient cet instant depuis le soir
        Où secouant le sable à la porte du jardin
        Tu apparus chantant des hymnes
        Nu comme ton sourire
        Auréolé du verbe
        Et je tendis la main en attendant
        Au fond des jours des nuages des jardins
        La neige fondre entre tes cils
        Les oiseaux entrer dans les arbres
        Le ciel se séparer des eaux
        Que tu me touches.

Dialogue

He says   I look at you like the image of myself
He says   I am the mirror and the two sides of the mirror

He says   You belong to me as I own myself
He says   I don't want to be yours or mine

He says   I enter as a meteorite and I burn your forests
He says   I am inside when I am outside

He says   I build you and I transform you
He says   What I have found I do not change

He says   I have but to touch you and we are one
He says

    I touch you and the sky separates itself from the waters
    Birds settle in the trees
    For they are waiting for that moment since the moment
    When pushing open the door of the days
    Birds settled in the trees
    Each one finding under a cloud the cloud
    Where it could gather its impatience and break it
    For they were waiting for that moment since the evening
    When shaking off the sand at the garden gate
    You arrived singing hymns
    Naked as your smile
    Haloed with words
    And I held out my hand waiting
    At the bottom of the days the clouds the gardens
    For the snow to melt between your lashes
    The birds to enter the trees
    The sky to separate itself from the water
    For you to touch me.

Retour des oiseaux

Retour des oiseaux quelque chose se passe là-haut
Aucun bruit ne parvient jusqu'à ce battement des ailes
Qui froisse le ciel pendant qu'en silence
Le noisetier gonfle ses chatons verts
Et que descend le dernier soleil hivernal
Jaune et rose derrière la brume lointaine.
Quelque chose se passe devant le disque déclinant
À une distance inappréciable jusqu'à ce que les hêtres
Frémissent du bruit d'ailes refermées
Et que caquètent dans la nuit qui s'installe
Et que commentent le voyage et l'asile enfin trouvé
Mille langues mille minuscules cervelles
Qui n'ont jamais connu cet arbre cette nuit
Et l'ont atteint pourtant comme nous revenons
Peut-être toujours à l'initiale hébétude
Heureux sans savoir ce qu'est le bonheur
De nous savoir là où nous ne savons pas où.

Return of the Birds

Return of the birds something's happening up there
No sound reaches that beating of wings
Which brush the sky while silently
The hazel tree inflates its green catkins
And the last sun of winter sets
Yellow and pink behind the distant haze.
Something's happening in front of the sinking disk
At an imperceptible distance until the beeches
Tremble with the sound of wings shut
And a thousand tongues
Chatter in the gathering night
Commenting on the journey and
The sanctuary found at last
And a thousand tiny brains
Who never knew that tree that night
And still found it as we come back
Perhaps always to the first stupor
Happy without knowing what happiness is
Knowing we are there where we don't know where we are.

Il est grand temps

Arriver tôt partir tard quand la nuit semble cracher ses plumes
Et ses poils voler l'ouate percer les arbres les murailles
D'un oeil d'or ouvert sous les phares.

Les monstres à roues blindées saccagent l'asphalte et les champs
Passage envahisseur de soldats bardés de zinc
Masqués comme la nuit les oreilles bouchées.

Une fois la porte fermée derrière moi je pris mon fouet
Le ciel lardé de giroflées séchait la lune quotidienne
Et le vent restait sourd aux explications cosmographiques.

Les tigres debout sur leur queue chantaient l'amour et le vin
Les abeilles cherchaient les fleurs de sang traces
De fleurs gorgées de vie sous les cicatrices.

Alors je laissai tomber un mot après un mot
Egrenant des sentences puisées à grande eau
Dans la sagesse toute neuve de mon âge

Après que de grands assassins nus postés au coin du papier peint
Loin de bergères évanouies de parallélogrammes abscons
Aient ouvert leur champ visuel pour capter mon haleine.

Vint le noir dessein des abrutis prendre ma main la serrer
Dans un étau dur comme l'ombre sous le roc mille vagues
Où silences et brouhahas attendent que la dernière fusée brûle

Et je m'allongeai enfin près d'un corps froid et m'endormis.

It's High Time

To arrive early leave late when night seems to spit out its feathers
And its hairs steal the wadding pierce the trees the wall
Of a golden eye open under the lighthouses.

Monsters with armored wheels pillage the asphalt and the fields
Invading passage of soldiers cased in zinc
Masked like night their ears stopped.

Once the door had shut behind me I took my whip
The sky studded with dianthus dried the daily moon
And the wind remained deaf to cosmographic explanations.

The tigers standing on their tails sang of love and wine
Bees sought out the flowers of blood traces
Of flowers glutted with life under the wounds.

So I let fall a word after a word
Reciting maxims fetched from deep water
In the brand-new wisdom of my age

After great naked assassins stationed at the corner of the wallpaper
Far from swooning shepherdesses from abstruse parallelograms
Had opened their field of vision to seize my breath.

Came the idiots' dark scheme to take my hand to press it
In a vise hard as shadow under the rock a thousand waves
Where silences and hubbubs wait for the last rocket to burn

And I lay down at last beside a cold body and went to sleep.

Lettre recommandée

Quand tu m'as téléphoné que tu arrivais de Freetown
Aussitôt j'étais à ta porte une bouteille d'arak au bras
Ton sourire s'irradia dans l'iris du judas

D'où te viennent à l'épaule ces félines ecchymoses
Sinon des grandes bêtes bleues poitrine huilée
Qui soufflent en riant sur les démons photophores

Une nuit noire et blanche et loin la robe de chambre
Je t'écrase lentement scarabée d'opale qui
Vénère un roi rayonnant et redoute ses porte-queues

C'est l'heure où le tonnerre à ma ceinture illumine
Ta lèvre occupée à baiser mes rotules
Le dos comme une mer coupable enfin châtiée

Puis tu m'as écrit de Bornéo: "J'ai montré ma peau zébrée au
Médecin du Bureau Central de Contrôle Sanitaire un grand
Singe poilu le kriss entre les dents fort intrigué."

Je sais quels cris s'étouffent aux moiteurs de la jungle
Et comment écorché tu gémis de plaisir plein la bouche
Et ce que cette tache sur ta lettre signifie.

Registered Letter

When you telephoned that you were arriving from Freetown
I was immediately at your door with a bottle of arak under my arm
Your smile was irradiated in the iris of the peephole

Where did you get those leopard bruises on your shoulder
If not from big blue beasts who are laughing
Blowing on demons in the dim light of photophores

A black and white night and off with the bathrobe
I hug you slowly opalescent scarab who worships
A shining king and fears his train bearers

This is the hour when thunder at my belt lights up
Your lips occupied in kissing my kneecaps
Your back like a guilty sea at last chastised

Then you wrote me from Borneo: "I have shown my zebra skin to
The Doctor of the Administration of Health, a big
Hairy ape with a kriss between his teeth, very intrigued."

I know what cries are choked in the clamminess of the jungle
And how when flayed you moaned your mouth full of pleasure
And what that stain on your last letter means.

The Landscape Is behind the Door

Ma Chandelle est morte

La chambre de ma mère a du papier à fleurs
Du papier à fleurs de papier
Ma mère avortera d'un prince rouge et noir
D'un gnome à la lèvre fendue
Mille raies bleues et jaunes enchantent mes réveils
Je reste le plus beau le plus sage
Je reste le meilleur des fils de ma mère
Et ma mère au profil dessiné sur le mur
Est sortie tôt pour boire des absinthes
Ou acheter du pain ou laver ma culotte
Ou vendre ma culotte et la sienne à personne
Souris au fromage rouge le temps passe
Souris ma soeur grise tu parles avec tes ongles
Un trou cache un piège
Un soir cache un jour
Un matin n'est jamais qu'une nuit fatiguée
De ce jour trop pareil au jour par la fenêtre.

Ma Chandelle est morte

My mother's bedroom has flowered wallpaper
Wallpaper with paper flowers
My mother will abort a black and red prince
A gnome with a harelip
A thousand blue and yellow stripes delight my wakings
I remain the handsomest the wisest
I remain the best of my mother's sons
And my mother with her profile drawn on the wall
Has gone out early to drink absinthe
Or buy bread or wash my underpants
Or sell my underpants and hers to no one
Mouse with red cheese time is passing
Mouse my gray sister you speak with your nails
A hole hides a trap
An evening hides a day
A morning is never anything but a tired evening
Of this day too much like the day beyond the window.

Ce que je dis, peut-être, n'est pas vrai

Les cinémas sont pleins d'ombres:
Un passé qui sera l'avenir permanent.
On entend parler des langues très anciennes
Des bouches un trait au crayon
Rouge restauré mille fois.
Et la chair vive et le coeur maltraité
La main qui cherche une main
Éprouvent de délicieux soulèvements
Immarcessibles
Un plaisir pareil à celui
Que donne la soif apaisée
Un soir
D'été trop lourd de joies.

Parmi les odeurs recréées
Un parfum venu de quelque
Lointain atavisme
Fait surgir sous la lumière démodée
Un décor comme un rêve
Décousu de tout réel
Dans lequel une fille un garçon
Si l'on en juge par leur voix
Se roulent sur une écharpe abandonnée
Cherchent la trace la sueur
Le passage d'un autre
Son amant son frère sa soeur
Lui-même
Sa raison d'être
Sa mort.

Les jours de pluie, puis
Un bateau sur l'horizon. La mer

What I Say, Perhaps, Isn't True

The cinemas are full of shadows:
A past that will be the permanent future.
One hears very ancient languages spoken
From mouths a red pencil line
Redrawn a thousand times.
And the living flesh and the abused heart
The hand that seeks a hand
Experience delightful
Incorruptible upheavals
A pleasure equal to the one that
Quenched thirst gives
On a summer evening
Too heavy with pleasures.

Among the recreated odors
A perfume arrived from some
Distant atavism
Causes scenery like a dream
To rise in the old-fashioned lighting
Unstitched from anything real
In which a girl a boy
To judge from their voices
Are rolling on an abandoned scarf
Searching for the trace the sweat
The passing of someone else
His lover his brother his sister
Himself
His reason for being
His death.

The days of rain then
A boat on the horizon. The sea

Sera un Sahara.
Et seul parmi les survivants déçus
Un enfant remplira de mémoire
Les pages,
Son œuvre millefeuille,
Le long déroulement de son
Calvaire (c'est trop dire).
Mais là, sans témoin ni
Complice, il fondra dans l'immensité
De l'instant,
Jusqu'à n'être plus qu'une
Goutte de cette pluie
Dans toute mer.

Will be a Sahara
And alone among the disappointed survivors
A child will fill the pages
With memory
His thousand-page opus,
The long unfolding of his
Calvary (that's too strong a word).
But there, with neither witness nor
Accomplice, he'll melt in the immensity
Of the instant,
Till he becomes just another
Drop of that rain
In that sea.

Sur le pont Marie

A qui le dire? Je crache des ronds
Je crache dans l'eau de la rivière
La nuit. Les épouvantes se rassemblent
Sans figure sans voix comme
Une absence qui ne commence pas.

La peur m'agrippe au parapet.
Pierre qui moud le grain de mon nom
Qui prolonge sa rigoureuse sensation
Le long des allers et retours
Sur le pont de chaque à chaque rive,
Refusant un chemin pour rentrer quelque part.

Savoir où je veux entrer sinon
Dans l'eau de cette rivière cette nuit
Par un crachat d'abord, puis une main
Qui lâche la pierre et bat le vide
Et griffe l'arche ouverte de la pierre dans l'eau,
Par mes cheveux affranchis de pesanteur
Dans ce saut, et mes yeux déchirant les couleurs renversées
Les signaux verts et rouges, flammes
Sous les cieux reflétés par les eaux.

Non je ne puis imaginer ma bouche suffocante
Mes poumons remplis d'eau
Ni la dernière image accrochée à mes yeux
L'instant où je la perds en cet instant
D'éternité finie à peine commencée.

A qui le dire? Je crache des ronds,
Je crache dans l'eau de la rivière la nuit.
Les épouvantes se rassemblent sans voix comme
Une absence qui ne finira pas.

On the Pont Marie

Who can I tell it to? I'm spitting rings
I'm spitting in the river water at night.
The terrors are gathering
Faceless voiceless like an absence
That doesn't begin.

Fear clamps me to the parapet.
Stone that mills the grain of my name pierre*
Prolonging its rigorous feeling
Along the comings and goings on the bridge
Of each to each bank,
Refusing a path that would lead somewhere like home.

To know where I want to go if not
Into the water of this river this night
First with a blob of spit, then a hand
That lets go of the stone and flails the empty air
And claws the empty arch between stone and water,
With my hair freed from gravity
Then with this leap and my eyes tearing the overturned colors
Green and red signals, flames
Under the sky reflected in the water.

No I can't imagine my mouth suffocating
My lungs swollen with water
Nor the last image fastened to my eyes
The instant I lose it in that instant
Of eternity ended when it's barely begun.

Who can I tell it to? I'm spitting rings,
I'm spitting in the river water at night.
The terrors are gathering voiceless like
An absence that won't end.

*One of several plays on the word pierre (stone) and Martory's first name.
(Trans.)

Dimanche et fêtes

Que l'on dédie ce jour au bonheur! J'ai monté
Des chevaux sur les airs d'un lointain opéra.
Ce manège et le ciel tournent comme la voix
Des enfants qui rient d'y être ensemble debout.

Abandonnons la ville à sa raideur de pierre
Ses bulbes ses plafonds ses rivières à ponts
Escaladons les toits jusqu'aux paratonnerres
Jusqu'au soleil tout nu que l'on touche du doigt.

Prenons congé des croix et des alléluias
Étouffons de baisers les sirènes guerrières
Offrons-nous pour fêter ce dimanche un bouquet de
Mille fleurs comme chants de cloches à midi.

Sundays and Holidays

May this day be dedicated to happiness! I have ridden
Horses to the tunes of a distant opera.
This carousel and the sky turn like the voice
Of children laughing to be there standing together.

Let's leave the city to its stony stiffness
Its bulbs its ceilings its rivers with bridges
Let's climb the roofs as far as the lightning-rods
As far as the naked sun you can touch with your finger.

Let's say farewell to crosses and alleluias
Let's smother the warrior sirens with kisses
To celebrate this Sunday let's buy ourselves a bouquet
Of a thousand flowers like songs of the bells at noon.

En bas des marches

C'était moi l'enfant dans la poussette
Qui descendait l'escalier d'Odessa.
Je criais, mais vous ne pouviez pas m'entendre
Puisque le film était muet.
Je hurlais: "A mort Bakounine! A mort
Le tsar et la flotte rouge! A mort
Celui qui inventa cette voiture pour bébés
Alors qu'il est si doux d'être porté
Endormi, de mourir peut-être
Sur le sein d'une femme aux joues roses et aux tresses jaunes! . . ."

Au pied des marches ils ramassèrent
Ma cervelle avec une cuillère d'argent.

Depuis ce jour je descends comme un fou
Toutes les marches d'escalier de vos vies,
Et je continue à crier: "À bas
Jéhovah, Jésus, Mahomet et autres fétiches
Qui prétendent ouvrir les portes de l'éternité!
À bas les grands hommes gavés d'arrogance
Qui instillent le fanatisme dans les coeurs!
À mort César, à bas la conquête du monde
À mort les révolutions l'argent le pouvoir!
Je veux un monde sans escaliers
Je veux dormir sur les rives de la mer Noire
Dans les bras d'une grosse grasse babouchka rose
Qui chante pour moi seul une berceuse."

At the Bottom of the Steps*

I was the child in the baby carriage
Rolling down the Odessa steps.
I cried, but you couldn't hear me
Because the film was silent.
I yelled: "Death to Bakunin! Death
To the czar and the red fleet! Death
To the inventor of this baby carriage
When it's so sweet to be carried,
Asleep, maybe dying,
On the bosom of a woman with pink cheeks and yellow braids! . . ."

At the bottom of the steps they scooped up
My brains with a silver spoon.

Since that day I roll like a lunatic
Down all the steps of the stairway of your lives,
And I go on screaming: "Down with
Jehovah, Jesus, Mohammed and other fetishes
Who claim to unlock the gates of eternity!
Down with the great men stuffed with arrogance
Who poison our hearts with fanaticism!
Death to Caesar, down with the conquest of the world,
Death to revolutions, money, power!
I want a world without stairs
I want to sleep on the shores of the Black Sea
In the arms of a fat pink babushka
Who'll sing a lullaby only to me."

*This title refers to Sergei Eisenstein's film *Battleship Potemkin*. (Trans.)

Le Paysage est derrière la porte

Le paysage est derrière la porte.
Le personnage est là . . . New York est plein
D'endroits pareils où se construit
Un monde, une nuée. Seules
Les têtes restent en place. On paye
Avant d'arriver, longtemps avant
D'ouvrir la bouche. Il y a près de nous
Des choses qui ont tous leurs côtés verts.

Les yeux se portent et se perdent.
Une chenille fait la différence.
La fille au sang plein le visage
S'arrête et demande l'heure.
C'est une année qui ne sait pas son nombre:
Un sourire au fond d'une poche.
Tiens! l'oiseau menteur frère des confidences
Quitte le lit familier des ruisseaux:
La vie des autres peinte sur la lampe.

"Je te touche comme une paye.
Tu es ma statue superflue
Couvée sous de chaudes larmes.
Je creuse jusqu'aux antipodes
Je déroule les bandelettes, l'horoscope:
C'est mon corps, c'est mon cocon, surpris
Dans un sommeil de sable prolifique
Que je découvre, cyclope évanoui."

Il suffirait d'entrer, de s'asseoir
Près d'un livre, de plier l'ombre
À ses genoux, de savoir qui
Marche sur le lit, passe le miroir.

The Landscape Is behind the Door

The landscape is behind the door.
The person is there ... New York is full
Of similar places where a world,
A large cloud, is being built. Only
The heads stay put. You pay
Before arriving, a long time before
Opening your mouth. There are things
Near us which all have their green sides.

You wear your eyes and lose them.
A caterpillar makes the difference.
The girl whose face is full of blood
Stops and asks the time.
It's a year that doesn't know its number:
A smile at the bottom of a pocket.
Look! the liar-bird, brother of secrets,
Leaves the familiar creek bed:
The life of others painted on a lampshade.

"I draw you like a salary.
You are my superfluous statue
Hatched beneath hot tears.
I'm digging toward the antipodes.
I unwind the bandages, the horoscope:
It's my body, it's my cocoon, surprised
In a sleep of prolific sand,
That I'm uncovering, like a Cyclops that fainted."

It would be enough to enter, to sit
Near a book, to fold the shadow
To one's knees, to know who
Walks on the bed, who passes the mirror.

La poussière grise le linge
Les photos étouffent de nuit.
Or rien n'apparaît dans la chambre
Sinon le paysage inaccessible dehors.

Là-bas, les feux de la préhistoire s'obstinent
À luire. La felouque égarée porte un squelette
À son tombeau. Un disque alimente le ciel.
Aux creux des geysers les dauphins
Profitent de l'incognito pour pleurer.
Une main religieuse étrangle la pitié
Et glisse dans la boîte aux lettres
La tristesse parfumée du silence.

La porte placardée de tels instants
Ne s'ouvre pas. Les cigarettes en fumée
Déroulées comme l'accessoire beauté
Laissent aux doigts l'odeur du temps passé.
L'intelligence géomètre arpente
La distance de dedans à dehors.
Tout est en place, rien ne manque.
De guerre lasse l'abeille contre
La vitre finit par renoncer à la fleur.

Dust tints the linens gray.
Photos choke on night.
Now nothing is visible in the room
Except the inaccessible landscape outdoors.

Down there, the fires of prehistory continue stubbornly
To glow. The lost felucca ferries a skeleton
To its grave. A disc feeds the sky.
In the hollows of geysers dolphins are taking
Advantage of their incognito to cry.
A pious hand is strangling the pity
And slips into the letterbox
The perfumed sadness of silence.

The door papered over with such moments
Doesn't open. The cigarettes unrolled
In smoke (a supplementary beauty)
Leave on the fingers the smell of time past.
Intelligence like a geometer paces
The distance from inside to outside.
Everything is in place, nothing is missing.
Weary of strife the bee on
The windowpane finally renounces the flower.

Sous l'orme

Sous l'orme depuis très longtemps
Je t'attends, ô mon âme.
Les semaines se suivent comme des livres
Qu'on parcourt la tête ailleurs
Pleine de musique elle aussi distraite
D'un profond bourdonnement où les mots les images
Les perceptions reposent dans le magma de mémoire
Dont est fait notre esprit.
Et rien ne vient affirmer ta venue,
Nul indice autre que fumée.
Est-ce toi qu'il aurait fallu accueillir
Quand la tendresse gonflait le coeur?
Toi qu'il fallait découvrir
Sur les rivages de la pitié ou de l'amour?
On ne m'a pas appris à reconnaître ta présence
Même quand les réveils soulèvent les membres
D'un bonheur à venir; même quand
Fatigué d'un long jour je cherche
Dans l'immense silence obscur où je bascule
Ce qui différencie le soleil de la mort.
Heures accumulées, richesse dérisoire,
Je suis prêt à quitter les arbres et les villes
Mais j'espère toujours te recevoir, mon âme,
Chargée de ma propre éternité.
Toi qui es moi, qui ne ressembles à personne,
Toi que je dois rendre un jour à qui sait qui.

Under the Elm

Under the elm for a long time
I've been waiting for you, O my soul.
Weeks follow each other like books
Perused, my thoughts elsewhere,
Full of music that's distracted too
Full of a deep buzzing where words images
Perceptions dwell in the jumble of memory
Of which our mind is composed.
And nothing comes to assert your coming
No other sign than smoke.
Is it you that we should have welcomed
When tenderness filled our hearts?
You that we should have discovered
On the shores of pity or of love?
I have not been taught to notice your presence
Even when reveille raises the limbs
Of a future happiness; even when
Tired of a long day I seek
Silence in the immense dark where I jettison
What differentiates the sun from death.
Hours accumulated, absurd riches,
I am ready to give up the trees and the cities
But I still hope to receive you, my soul,
Laden with my own eternity.
You who are me, who resembles nobody,
You that I must give back some day to who knows who.

Dune

"Les cygnes amputés de leurs ailes violettes"
Disais-tu, en jetant les pages aux roseaux
D'un livre: *Mrs Dalloway.*
L'herbe nue battait un cadre de papier doré
La moisissure. C'était une vignette à peine vierge
Sous la pluie. Et soudain
Ni toi ni moi n'étions plus là ou pas encore.
Nous avions disparu derrière la plus haute dune d'Europe
Elle-même se déplaçant dans l'espace et le temps
Grain de sable après grain de sable.

Je me suis roulé sur tes mains,
J'ai léché tes genoux, ton ventre. La bouche
Pleine de galets j'ai cessé de bégayer
Mon nom. Il me semblait que le sable
Tremblait derrière moi sous des pas.
Je me retournais. Derrière moi
Personne, sinon toi qui criais, "Es-tu là?"

J'étais là.

L'arbre au lointain pencha un peu sous le vent.
La fumée des vapeurs, le parfum des pins écrasés . . .
Un nid creusé sous mon aisselle:
L'oiseau y dépose ses oeufs.
Je les couve, tenus par des sangles cruelles
Et mon sang gicle sous ma peau.
C'est là la blessure que je me suis faite
En cherchant la blessure que tu m'as faite.

Les pavillons glissent devant la fenêtre
Le soleil tombe dans la coupe de jaspe.
Un très lent crissement de métal mouillé . . .

Demain il fera beau dit la radio.

Dune

"The swans with their purple wings amputated"
You said, throwing to the reeds pages
Of a book: *Mrs. Dalloway.*
The naked grass was beating a gilt frame on a page:
Mildew. It was a barely virgin text illustration
In the rain. And suddenly
Neither I nor you were there or not yet.
We had disappeared behind the highest dune in Europe
The dune itself moving into space and time
Grain after grain of sand.

I have rolled around on your hands,
I have licked your knees, your belly. My mouth
Full of pebbles I have stopped stuttering
My name. It seemed to me that the sand
Was trembling behind me under footfalls.
I turned around. Behind me
No one, unless you who cried, "Are you there?"

I was there.

The distant tree bent a little in the wind.
The steamers' smoke, the perfume of trodden pine needles . . .
A nest hollowed under my armpit:
The bird leaves its eggs there.
I hatch them, fastened by cruel bands
And my blood spurts under my skin.
There is the wound I gave myself
While I was looking for the wound you gave me.

The ship's pennants are gliding past the window
The sun is sinking in the jasper cup.
A very slow squeaking of wet metal . . .

Tomorrow the weather will be fair says the radio.

Un Dimanche à Monfort l'Amaury

Un oeuf vert couvé sous la neige
Un oeuf couvert d'idéogrammes

Si le petit train stoppe aux marges des cartes
N'en profite pas pour filer par le trou de la baignoire

L'artiste rétablit sur le gazon
Son équilibre perdu aux grilles du balcon

Nous avions vu ensemble les pires paysages
Regrettant le noir et blanc du cinématographe

Quand nous rentrions plus loin du chien que près du loup
Personne pour nous accueillir à grands coups de courroux

À Cadix pour mieux écouter les castagnettes
Nous avions meurtri nos mains à quelques espagnolettes

La lune ravageant d'exquises mosaïques
Gardait le moelleux de flûtes maghrébines

Aujourd'hui tinte encore à l'abri des curieux
L'argentin boléro d'un cymbalum quinteux

Le retour s'effectua par une nuit incommensurable
Peuplée de chats enroués d'Anglaises lasses

Un rideau dont la soie brûle
Ne cache plus qu'un souvenir ridicule

Un oeuf vert couvé sous la neige
Un oeuf couvert d' idéogrammes.

A Sunday in Monfort l'Amaury

A green egg incubating under the snow
An egg covered with ideograms

If the little train stops at the maps' margins
Don't seize the chance to escape down the bathtub drain

The acrobat re-establishes on the lawn
The balance he lost on the balcony railing

Together we had seen the worst landscapes
Regretting the cinematographer's black and white

When we came back, far from the dog, close to the wolf's path,*
There was no one to welcome us with great bursts of wrath

At Cádiz, the better to hear the castanets,
We bruised our hands grappling with some espagnolettes

The moon, laying waste to exquisite mosaics
Still kept the mellowness of Maugrabin flutes

Today, shielded from inquisitive comers,
The Argentine bolero still tinkles on catarrhal dulcimers

The return was accomplished on an incommensurable night
Peopled with hoarse-voiced cats and weary Englishwomen

A curtain whose silk is ablaze
Conceals nothing more than a stupid lost phrase

A green egg incubating under the snow
An egg covered with ideograms

* *"Entre chien et loup"* (halfway between dog and wolf) is a common French expression for twilight, a time when it would be difficult to distinguish between a wolf and a dog seen from a distance. (Trans.)

La Cage

Etes-vous entré dans la cage? La plus vide?
Soudain tout glisse de l'autre côté sans à-coup:
Les arbres, les maisons, les promeneurs, les journaux;
Soudain tout est balayé de ses couleurs accoutumées,
Le sens des vents, le déroulement des après-midi;
Soudain tout est oublié: la géométrie, la poésie,
Le poids du coeur, les racines, les années.
Seule s'installe une splendide faim de forêt vierge
Et c'est elle qui vous pousse à sortir de la cage.

Vous n'êtes plus le même désormais,
Pas même dans votre lit, dans les bras d'une femme,
Pas même dans vos rêves où vous arpentez un désert
Tout parcouru du fumet des gazelles;
Pas même dans la contemplation en vous de ce phénomène étrange
Dont vous perdez conscience et qui ne signifie rien pour vous.

Tout est oublié, la cage et le bâillement immense de la foule,
Et la satisfaction incalculable d'être là où il faut.

The Cage

Have you gone into the cage? The emptiest one?
Suddenly everything slides to the other side without jarring:
Trees, buildings, pedestrians, newspapers;
Suddenly everything is swept clean of its habitual colors
The direction of the winds, the unrolling of afternoons;
Suddenly everything is forgotten: geometry, poetry,
The weight of the heart, the roots, the years.
Only a splendid virgin-forest hunger moves in
And it's that that makes you leave the cage.

Henceforth you're no longer the same,
Not even in your bed, in a woman's arms,
Not even in your dreams where you stride across a desert
Traversed by the scent of gazelles;
Not even in the contemplation in you of this strange phenomenon
Of which you lose consciousness and which means nothing to you.

Everything is forgotten, the cage and the immense yawn of the crowd,
And the incalculable satisfaction of being right where you belong.

Prose de Buttes-Chaumont

L'auteur des ces jardins se jeta, prétends-tu,
Du haut du Temple de l'Amour, copie
Du Douglas Stewart Monument, Carlton Hill, Édimbourg,
Sauf que sur le socle ici, au centre de la colonnade,
Le petit dieu, invisible d'ailleurs sur la vue
Stéréoscopique de référence, est absent,
Prêt à être remplacé sans doute le temps d'un déclic
Par un enfant venu contempler un dimanche,
Comme nous, le panorama crevé de brumes,
La ville peinte sur un frémissement du temps.

Mais la question n'est pas là.

Je voulais te saisir la main
Et d'un coup de talon prendre essor avec toi
Comme les figures de Puvis de Chavannes
Dans Le Bois sacré cher aux Muses et aux Arts
Ou comme dans ces rêves dont nous parlions,
Où, marchant dans la foule, il suffit d'un pas plus long
Pour nous hisser au ras des têtes en évitant les becs de gaz
Les isolateurs de verre, les poteaux, les girouettes.

Comment reçoit-il ma ville, ton regard
Encore accroché à la frange hispanique de Riverside Park
Ou du côté du Flatiron?
Et moi, le sac lourd de science livresque—
Flasque butin volé aux poubelles de l'Histoire—
Qu'est-ce-que je vois qui n'est pas dans tes yeux?

Des portes à guichet
Des enseignes bleuies
Un ange bardé de cuir

Prose des Buttes-Chaumont

The creator of these gardens threw himself—so you claim—
From the top of the Temple of Cupid, a copy
Of the Douglas Stuart monument, Carlton Hill, Edinburgh,
Except that here, on the pedestal at the center of the colonnade,
The diminutive god, invisible in fact on the stereopticon
View I am consulting, is missing,
Ready to be replaced no doubt in the instant of a shutter's click
By a child who like us has come, on a Sunday,
To gaze at the fog-pierced panorama,
The city painted on a tremor of time.

But that's not the issue.

I wanted to grab your hand and touch bottom
So we can take off into space together
Like the figures in Puvis de Chavannes'
The Sacred Wood Beloved of the Muses and the Arts
Or like those dreams we were talking about,
Where, walking in a crowd, we have only to take a giant step
To fly away, grazing heads as we avoid the street lamps,
The glass insulators on telegraph poles, the weather vanes.

How does it digest my city, your look
Still lingering on the hispanic fringe of Riverside Park,
Or down by the Flatiron?
And I, with my sackful of bookish knowledge—
Flaccid booty stolen from the trash cans of History—
What do I see that's not in your eyes?

Gates with turnstiles
Bluish neon
A leather angel

Avec sa chaine en argent
Porté par des nuées
De Gitanes papier maïs
Qui examine s'il y a
Des rides autour de nos yeux
Avant de nous percer
Le ventre d'un laser…?

Une rue parcourue par d'étranges messages
Que s'envoient les voyous à travers la cervelle
En carton bouilli perméable d'un flic …?

Un flot d'alcool berçant
De ses graves volutes
Des baisers que nous finirons par échanger …?

Un livre commencé manuscrit par un moine
Et achevé sur l'écran d'un ordinateur
Dans une langue talée comme figues trop mûres
Où croupit une odeur d'alphabet mal connu …?

Une femme fanée fumant dans les décombres
Sans hâte sachant bien que tout désir est mort
Serre-t-elle en sa main une graine germée
Espoir d'un arbre de la Science du Bien et du Mal …?

La rue en bas peut conduire au quai
Le quai aboutit toujours à une chambre
La chambre est toujours occupée par un lit
Le lit n'a de place que pour ton corps
Ton corps se réduit à ta bouche
Toutes les mains se posent sur des cuisses.
Enveloppons-nous de brouillards mauves.
C'est la nuit des parfums et je découvre
En m'approchant de ton bas-ventre
La place exacte où vont foisonner les cloportes.

With his silver chain
Borne on clouds
Of maize-paper Gitanes
Looking to see whether there are
Wrinkles around our eyes
Before stabbing our
Bellies with a laser . . . ?

A street traversed by odd messages
From punk to punk across the porous
Porridge of a cop's brain . . . ?

A wave of alcohol cradling
In its solemn scrolls
Kisses we will one day exchange . . . ?

A book begun in manuscript by a monk
And finished on the screen of a computer terminal
In a bruised language like overripe figs
Where the perfume of a little-known alphabet stagnates . . . ?

A faded woman who's smoking amid the rubble,
Not in haste, knowing well that all desire is dead;
Does she clasp a sprouted seed,
The hope of a tree of Knowledge of Good and Evil . . . ?

The street below probably leads to the embankment
The embankment always ends in the bedroom
The bedroom is always filled up by the bed
The bed has room only for your body
Your body is reduced to your mouth
All hands are placed on thighs.
Let's wrap ourselves in lavender fog.
It's the night of perfumes and I discover
As I approach your groin
The exact spot where wood lice will swarm.

Je te donne Paris ses paires d'yeux ses coeurs
Chacun gros comme un poing de boxeur.
Écoute: ils accordent leur battement
Dans le ronron du silence.
Je te donne, ajoutant parole sur parole,
Les milliards de mots prononcés à cet instant.
Regarde: un seul cristal liquide c'est ton nom.
Je te donne la fournaise des corps jetés
Dans la gueule du temps. Touche:
La peau humaine électrise tes doigts.
Tout est à toi.
Remets en sortant ton ticket de vestiaire
Personne ne criera au voleur.
La porte refermée, le ciel toujours de soufre
Roulera par tes nuits et tes nuits
Ajoutant aux images mortes des images.

De quoi est fait ce paysage des hommes
Auquel tu appartiens?
Tu t'y promènes avec moi
Sans en éprouver un vertige.
Tu es trop sûr que les abîmes
Où se perdent en bas les autres
Pour nous ne l'ouvriront pas.

This poem and translation first appeared in *Every Question but One*. (Eds.)

I give you Paris its pairs of eyes its hearts
Each as big as a boxer's fist.
Listen: they're synchronizing their heartbeats
In the hum of silence.
I give you—adding speech to speech—
The billions of words pronounced at this instant.
Look: a single liquid crystal and it's your name.
I give you the furnace of bodies thrown
Into the jaws of time. Touch:
Human skin electrifies your fingers.
Everything is yours
Return your coat check as you leave
No one will cry thief.
Once the door is shut the sky, still sulfur,
Will roll through your nights and your nights
Adding images to dead images.

What is it made of, this landscape of men
To which you belong?
You walk there with me,
Feeling no vertigo.
You're too sure that the abysses
In which the others are lost down there
Won't open for us.

Archives indéchiffrables

Dans cette maison où personne n'habite
Les portes s'ouvrent sur des horizons cadenassés
Les arbres peints en noir résonnent du silence
D'oiseaux desséchés attendant la résurrection
Pour peu qu'un vent suffisant souffle sur leur plumage
Révélant leur couleur leur espèce et leur sexe.

L'air pourtant imprégné d'imprécises présences
Conserve le parfum de vies anciennes oubliées
Dans des tiroirs aux serrures que gardent
(Lèvres serrées roses confites dans la glace)
Des secrets attendant d'improbables baisers
Pour mordre à mort celui qui voudrait les violer

Et demander: où sont parties les âmes immortelles?
Celle qui regardait le soir se balancer les bateaux
Celle qui brûlait sa chair pour un inaccessible amour.

Il y a quelque part dans une grotte dans un désert
Une brique d'argile marquée au coin d'un alphabet
Qui nous dirait comment le silence pesait
Au musicien privé de son orgue
Et si les larmes de l'amant délaissé
Avaient les couleurs de nos prières
Et si un coeur battait de la même angoisse haletante
Que le nôtre le soir quand sonne une cloche au lointain.

Undecipherable Archives

In that house where no one lives
The doors open on padlocked horizons
The black-painted trees echo with the silence
Of dessicated birds awaiting resurrection
If enough wind ever blows on their plumage
Revealing their color their species their sex.

The air nevertheless permeated with imprecise presences
Keeps the perfume of forgotten former lives
In drawers with locks that hold
(Clenched lips roses candied in ice)
Secrets awaiting unlikely kisses
So as to bite to death the one who would violate them

And ask: where have the immortal souls gone?
The one that looked at the boats swaying at evening
The one that burned its flesh for an inaccessible lover.

There is somewhere in a cave in a desert
A clay brick stamped with an alphabet
That would tell us how the silence weighed
On the musician deprived of his clavier
And if the tears of the abandoned lover
Were the color of our prayers
And if a heart was beating with the same breathless anguish
As ours when a distant bell sounds in the evening.

Urbs

De mes semelles mille pluies j'étale sur le macadam,
Bouillie de sang d'épinards d'oeufs malades,
L'alphabet mouvant du néon.
Couchée près de ce bois qu'elle prend pour son dieu,
Fille folle sincèrement d'être éternelle,
La ville s'offre en ses reflets d'hiver toujours
Chapelet de martyrs au cou, l'oeil de fumées.

Souviens-toi de Rome de Rome de Rome.
Colonnes sans feuillages autres que les flèches
Pour Sébastien déshabillé par quelque guide;
Voûtes rompues où le ciel bat des étincelles;
La cigarette à la bouche rouge, un abbé
Regrette de païens baisers sans contrition,
Cris béats, pages roses d'un Larousse en toutes langues.

Si proches parentes cités successives
Qui ne se disent rien mais se ressemblent.
Corps corrompu où boivent leur vraie vie
Les mouches à l'échelle des fresques éteintes.
Brocart mité des vierges en majesté.
Sages saintes au regard de plâtre.
Tant d'os dorment ici dans un magasin de piété.

Souviens-toi de Rome de Rome de Rome.
La nuit contre les manches en croix d'un vieil ange,
Contre un Antinoüs et son sexe élimé,
Contre Adrien pleurant derrière une chapelle,
Contre les voix hurlant à la mort d'un géant,
Les mille yeux crevés, les fausses ombres, les secrets,
Un cirque pour toujours péripatétique et sonore.

Urbs

With my soles I stir up a thousand rains on the asphalt
Gruel of blood of spinach of sick eggs
The blinking alphabet of neon.
Lying near the wood that she mistakes for a god
Girl sincerely mad to be eternal,
The city offers itself in its winter reflections always
Chaplet of martyrs at its throat, eye of smoke.

Remember Rome Rome Rome.
Columns with no other foliage than arrows
For Sebastian undressed by some guide;
Broken vaults where the sky beats sparks;
Cigarette at his red mouth, a priest
Longs for pagan kisses without contrition,
Blissful cries, pink pages of a Larousse in all languages.

Such near relations successive cities
Who don't speak to each other but resemble each other.
Putrid body where flies on the same scale as erased frescoes
Drink their real life.
Moth-eaten brocade of the virgins in splendor.
Wise saints with plaster gazes.
So many bones asleep here in a shop of religious images.

Remember Rome Rome Rome.
Night against the crossed sleeves of an old angel
Against an Antinous with worn genitals
Against Hadrian weeping behind a chapel
Against voices howling at the death of a giant
The thousand eyes put out, the false shadows, the secrets,
An echoing arena where tourists stroll forever.

Souviens-toi de ces trous, des coupoles qui les comblent,
Des crânes embaumés, des bijoux qui les ornent,
Des oliviers jaunis sous le coca-cola,
De tes pas dans les pas d'actuels somnambules
Pressés de retrouver au détour d'un palais
Une borne où laisser leurs gants et leur sourire
Pour nager nus dans la Cloaca Maxima.

Remember those holes the cupolas that fill them,
The embalmed skulls, the jewels that decorate them,
The yellowing olive trees under the Coca-Cola,
Your footsteps in the steps of today's sleepwalkers
Anxious to find in the angle of a palace
A milestone on which they can leave their gloves and their smile
And swim naked in the Cloaca Maxima.

Dans le ventre de la baleine

Air respiré sans le savoir,
Agréable balancement doublé
D'une musique, un rêve, qui sait?
Et l'impression d'être en dehors
Du temps à attendre
Sans fin l'accomplissement
Des choses.
Sommeil éternel, durant juste
Un oisif matin, sans
Références aux visions à venir,
Aux nuits perdues.

A travers les liquides distances
S'entendent pourtant
Comme rugissements étouffés
La rumeur d'hommes traînant sur les plages
Garçons dont l'errance empoisonne les soirs.
Ils n'entendent plus la langue qu'ils parlent
Ils pleurent comme des chiens
En regardant tomber la lune
Dans cet horizon où je baigne.
Ils dévorent leur propre chair
Et font l'amour puis lacèrent leur sexe
Les yeux fermés car ils n'avaient plus de désirs.
Ils dansent parmi l'univers bousculé
Le frénétique pas des espoirs scalpés . . .

Sont-ils donc, ceux-là, mes semblables?
Et Seigneur suis-je sur les mêmes vagues
A me vautrer comme une truie gravide
Sur les tripes pestilentielles,
Secouée par les borborygmes

In the Belly of the Whale

Air breathed in without my knowing it,
Pleasant swaying that rhymes
With a certain music, a dream, who knows?
And the impression of being outside
Of time to await
Endlessly the completion
Of things.
Eternal sleep lasting only
An idle morning without
Reference to the visions to come,
To the lost nights.

Through the liquid expanses
However one can still hear
Something like a stifled roar
The noise of men loitering on the beaches
Boys whose wandering poisons the evenings.
They no longer hear the language they speak
They weep like dogs
Watching the moon fall
Into the horizon that bathes me.
They devour their own flesh
And make love then lacerate their cocks
With their eyes closed for they had no more desires.
They dance amid the jostled universe
The frantic dance of scalped hopes . . .

Are *they* then my fellow creatures?
And Lord am I on the same waves
Wallowing like a gravid sow
On pestilential tripe,
Shaken by rumbling bowels

Que je croyais cordes suaves
Au flanc d'un coeur hypertrophié
Qui bat un tam-tam angélique? Suis-je
À glisser jusqu'à la matrice
Écrin clos où le temps attend
Sans fin l'accomplissement
Des choses?

I thought were suave ropes
In the flank of a hypertrophied heart
Beating an angelic tom-tom? Am I
To slip as far down as the womb
Shut jewel-case where time awaits
Endlessly the completion
Of things?

Blues

La voie du chemin de fer me lie à ces jours d'enfer
La voie du chemin de fer une seule nuit peut tout faire

Amour des autres tu m'uses à grands coups de brosse dure

Dans une gare de Paris est-ce l'amour qui sourit?
Dans une gare de Paris tout commence et tout finit.

Amour des autres tu suces le jeune sang de ma vie

Et les mots de mon grand frère que j'entends encore dans mon lit
Et les mots de mon grand frère se peut-il qu'il les oublie?

Amour des autres tu tardes à promettre récompense.

Ainsi soit-il mon enfant y en a qui sont pas contents
Ainsi soit-il mon enfant on gagne on perd tout le temps

Amour des autres tu crèves mes yeux à force de fièvres.

Adieu c'est un grand mouchoir un grand mouchoir de papier
Qu'on jette à l'égout après que les larmes l'ont souillé.

Amour des autres tu laisses dans la bouche un goût de glaise.

Blues

The bed of the railway links me to these days of hell
The bed of the railway just one night can do it all

Love of the others you wear me out with great strokes of a stiff brush

In a station of Paris is there a true love that smiles?
In a station of Paris everything begins and everything fails.

Love of the others you suck the young blood of my life

And the words of my big brother I can still hear them on my cot
And the words of my big brother can it be he forgot?

Love of the others you are slow to promise a reward.

So be it my child some people are never satisfied
So be it my child some win some fall by the wayside

Love of the others you put out my eyes by dint of fevers.

Goodbye is a big handkerchief a big handkerchief of paper
That you throw in the sewer once it's been soiled with tears.

Love of the others you leave in my mouth a taste of clay.

Quatorze Millions d'années-lumière

Oubliés tout à l'heure et demain
Éclate dans un bruit que nulle oreille ne perçoit
Le commencement de la fin
Puisque tout ce qui commence finit
L'univers comme une ligne comme ce poème une vie
Connaître son père et sa mère et leurs pères

Savoir qu'au plus lointain calendrier
Le corps d'un animal si monocellulaire
Qu'il n'a laissé de trace dans les couches profondes
Se trouve attiré par son semblable,
Qu'il a fallu être deux pour être un . . .

Love-toi près de moi mon ventre épouse ton dos
Une autre nuit défilera quand nous dormons
Et si nous dormons quelle nuit infinie
Où nulle question ne sera posée
Nulle théorie ne surgira de nos songes?

Tiens ma main rejoignons ensemble
L'oubli de l'heure et de demain
Du grand commencement de toutes choses qui finissent
Corps flagellé oeuf unis dans la nuit infinie
Toute vérité pourrait nourrir nos mensonges
Love-toi près de moi dormons ensemble.

Fourteen Million Light-Years

Now that See you later and tomorrow are forgotten
The beginning of the end
Explodes into a sound that no ear perceives
Since everything that begins ends
The universe like a line like this poem a life
To know one's father and one's mother and their fathers

To know that on the farthest calendar
The body of an animal so monocellular that it
Left no trace in the deep strata
Finds itself attracted to its fellow,
To know that it was necessary to be two in order to be one . . .

Coil up next to me my stomach fits your back
Another night will pass while we sleep
And if we sleep what infinite night
Wherein no question will be asked
No theory rise out of our dreams.

Hold my hand let's go back together
To the forgetting of the hour and tomorrow
Of the great beginning of all things that end
Flagellar body joined with the egg in endless darkness
Every truth could nurture our lies
Coil up next to me let's sleep together.

Après l'orage

Maintenant pour partir
La lune est trop basse.
On atteint la plage à la marche
Une heure passée avec les tarots
A cassé le jour en deux miroirs
Images mouillées racines dénudées
Chevelures offertes aux dernières
Goulées du vent liant les mains.

Assise la frileuse au feu de sa croix
Attend que la nuit la saisisse.
Les roseaux chuintent mâts scintillants.
Dans le portefeuille parmi les photos de noyés
Décapités par les myriapodes,
Un loup se transforme en soupirs
Ainsi parfois dans la forêt pleurent
Les lionnes un psaume, un mot perdus.

Le cri au retour de l'oiseau
Annonce d'épaisses rencontres
Alors la langue que percent les dents
Ne demande plus quel chemin conduit
Au sable abreuvé de salive.
Le coeur sèche avec le rivage.
L'espoir s'engloutit dans la nuit.
La lune monte l'implacable.

After the Storm

Now the moon is too low
For us to leave
We get to the beach on foot
An hour spent with the tarot cards
Has broken the day into two mirrors
Wet images roots laid bare
Tresses offered to the last
Mouthfuls of wind tying our hands together

The woman sitting by the fire of her cross feels cold
Waits for night to seize her.
Reeds shushing masts sparkling.
In the wallet amid photos of drowned people
Decapitated by centipedes and millipedes,
A wolf transforms himself into sighs
So sometimes in the forest lionesses
Weep for a lost psalm, a lost word.

The cry at the bird's return
Announces thick encounters
It's then that the tongue pierced by teeth
No longer asks which road leads
To the sand slaked with saliva.
The heart dries out with the shore.
Hope sinks into night.
The moon the implacable rises.

Diamant noir

La paisible harmonie d'un dimanche matin
Plein de couleurs d'un apparent silence,
Le paysage dehors vert et bleu, le soleil
Caché derrière l'occasionnel carillon d'une église
Et dans la chambre une présence qui s'en va,
Un au revoir flottant dans l'air comme
Le dernier ruban d'une fumée de cigarette . . .

La porte fermée on se retrouve devant la mer
Miroir qui ne reflète ni la fenêtre ni le monde
Brutalement impénétrable où l'on peut peindre toutefois
L'obscur le fulgurant et les deux infinis
Les musiques les mots l'irréel et le vrai
Le souffle de la vie éphémère buée
Le coeur brûlant brûlé aux feux d'un diamant noir.

Il y a un lit dans toutes nos journées
Une chute soudaine, une difficile descente.
Toujours autant de jours que nous vivons
Dans l'heure où nous quittons le jour, pour commencer
L'apprentissage jamais accompli de la nuit.

Stagnent dans ce loisir de notre veille d'autres
Tableaux qui nous égarent, paysages rompus, visages
Oubliés et les monstres de nos précédentes rencontres
Avec les images que nous renvoie le mur de notre chambre
Face à la fenêtre dont il n'est pas le reflet.

Le jardin clos d'iris et de roses de Sharon
L'eau du bassin où s'ébroue le gras rouge-gorge
Le sifflet du train, la campagne jusqu'au fleuve
La pleine lune et ses tourbillons de nuée bleue

Black Diamond

The peaceful harmony of a Sunday morning
Filled with the colors of an apparent silence,
The landscape outside green and blue, the sun
Hidden behind the occasional chiming from a church
And in the bedroom a presence that is leaving,
A goodbye floating in the air like
The last ribbon of cigarette smoke . . .

Once the door has shut one is back before the sea
Mirror that reflects neither the window nor the world
Brutally impenetrable where one can nonetheless paint
The dark the flashing and the two infinities
The musics the words the unreal and the true
The breath of life fleeting vapor
The burning heart burnt in the sparkle of a black diamond.

There is a bed in all our days
A sudden fall, a difficult descent
Always as many days as we live
In the hour when we leave day to begin the never finished
Apprenticeship of night.

Stagnating in this leisure of our vigil other
Pictures lose us, broken landscapes, forgotten
Faces and the monsters of our previous meetings
With the images the bedroom wall beams back to us
Facing the window of which it is not the reflection.

The enclosed garden of iris and rose of Sharon
The water in the birdbath where the fat robin fusses
The train whistle, the country down to the river
The full moon and its eddies of blue cloud

Toute la terre et nous seuls à savoir que nous dormons
Toujours seuls, une fois les paupières fermées,
Et le néant qui achèvera de durer . . .

All the earth and only we to know that we sleep
Always alone, once our eyelids are shut,
And the nothingness which will leave off lasting . . .

Capsule

War ein Haus wo, da warst du drein
Und die Leute schicken mich herein.

Hugo von Hofmannsthal
Der Rosenkavalier

J'essayai désespérément de penser à quelque chose
Qui ne m'était encore jamais venu à l'esprit
Et ce fut d'entrer dans un tube d'aluminium
Comprimé d'aspirine ou cigare. Je me desséchais
N'attendant plus la pluie dans cet espace confiné—
Situation étrange mais on en voit de pire
Dans les films d'horreur.
                              Or il plut. Il suffisait
D'y croire avec force, une fois entré dans le tube.
Of course!
                    Vous ignorerez toujours la puissance
Et la résistance du vouloir avant de sentir
Comme une lézarde dans l'air comprimé autour de vous
L'air lui-même comme un mur. Le jour comme une lézarde
Au fond d'un puits. Et que ce que vous preniez
Pour une vague sur quoi rouler votre paresse,
Comme dans l'abîme minuscule fragment, une cloche à plongeur.
Oui. Au commencement est la lézarde
L'échelle. Puis l'effort pour deviner si l'on est
À la surface de la paroi ou sous la cloche.
Ding ding dong. C'est le même son.
Vous vous balancez au fanon d'Apis
Vous vous desséchez dans la capsule d'aluminium
Vous attendez désespérément la pluie
La moindre goutte de changement.

Capsule

War ein Haus wo, da warst du drein
Und die Leute schicken mich herein.

Hugo von Hofmannsthal
Der Rosenkavalier

I was trying desperately to think of something
That had never occurred to me before
And it was to enter an aluminum tube
Like the ones for aspirin or cigars. I was drying up,
No longer expecting rain in that narrow space—
Curious situation but you see worse ones
In horror movies.

                Well, it was raining. It was enough
To believe it, forcefully, once I was inside the tube.
Of course!

             You'll never know the power
And the resistance of the will until you feel
Like a crevice in the compressed air around you
The air itself like a wall. Daylight like a crevice
At the bottom of a well. And what you mistook
For a wave on which to roll your laziness,
A diving bell, miniscule fragment in the abyss.
Yes. In the beginning is the crevice
The ladder. Then the effort to find out if one is
On the surface of the partition or under the bell.
Ding ding dong. It's the same sound.
You dangle from the dewlap of Apis
You dry out in the aluminum capsule
You wait desperately for rain
The least drop of change.

Lac rouge et noir

Poème démodé

Fulgurances silencieuses échappant au temps
Rubans de lumière soudain donnant vie aux ténèbres
À l'horizon griffé d'éclairs, et sur les vagues dont la présence
Se trahissait par un humide clapotis aveuglant
Étendue obscure alourdie de caoutchouc d'huiles visqueuses
Commencements sans témoins du monde

Une à une les voitures s'arrêtent feux éteints
Radios fermées. On n'entend pas les oiseaux dit une femme
On n'entend pas le tonnerre c'est curieux dit un homme
Il cherche la main rassurante d'un enfant
Ils avancent sur la plage herbeuse
Il me semble qu'il fait froid dit un vieillard

Et peu à peu mais à la vitesse d'un songe
S'embrase le panorama jusqu'à révéler
De grands pans de paysage sur la rive lointaine
Tels qu'on ne les vit jamais par le jour le plus clair
Qui disparaissent et renaissent dans le grondement
Continu comme d'une bête qui s'éveille

Les déchirures de néant le flamboiement des eaux
Le crépitement différé de gigantesques étincelles
La couleur révélée du ciel en feu
Le bruit l'odeur de l'eau agitée
Et le tonitruant vacarme coupé
De brefs silences électriques

L'orage roule sur le lac le lac rougeoie
Le monde croule de nuées noires

Red and Black Lake

Old-fashioned poem

Silent flashes escaping from time
Ribbons of light suddenly bringing the shadows to life
On the horizon scrawled with lightning, and on the waves whose presence
Is revealed by a damp blinding plashing
Dim expanse weighted with rubber with viscous oils
Unwitnessed beginnings of the world

One by one the cars stop their lights off
Their radios off. You don't hear the birds says a woman
You don't hear the thunder it's strange says a man
He reaches for a child's reassuring hand
They move forward on the grassy beach
It seems to me that it's cold says an old man

And little by little but at the speed of a dream
The panorama catches fire until it reveals
Enormous landscape panels on the distant shore
As one never saw them before in brightest daylight
That disappear and are reborn in the continual
Growling like that of an animal waking

The rents in nothingness the flaming of the waters
The deferred sputtering of gigantic sparks
The revealed color of the fiery sky
The sound the smell of the churning water
And the thundering racket cut
By brief electric silences

The storm rolls on the lake the lake reddens
The world collapses from black clouds

Le vent qui se lève rabat les voix
De grosses gouttes claquent sur les pare-brise
Puis la pluie se déchaîne en longues draperies
Qui se retroussent sur l'asphalte au feu des phares

The rising wind beats down the voices
Big drops slap the windshield
Then the rain breaks loose in long curtains
That tuck themselves up from the asphalt in the glare of the headlights

Pêle-mêle

Une voix qui dit: "Vous l'avez voulu"
Et la même chambre au matin suivant.

Une autre qui dit: "Il ne fallait pas"
Et sa résonance au cours des années.

Un enfant qui dit: "Je ne puis aimer"
Un adulte écoute et ne comprend pas.

Un soldat qui pleure au bord d'un oued
Un autre qui rit en mourant pour rien.

La lettre à portée des regards curieux
Qui n'apprenait rien qu'on ne sût déjà.

Un après-midi de quatorze juillet
Ce feu d'artifice au-dessous des toits.

Un train de minuit pour Dieppe et Le Havre
Et deux innocents rêvant l'Amérique.

En hâte avalée aspirine hostie
Et ce mal de coeur qui n'en finit pas.

La foule en liesse un rapide adieu
Un mot souligné dans le dictionnaire.

L'escalier rayon des coeurs esseulés
L'appel d'un regard qu'on ne verra plus.

Ternis sous la poussière et la vitre salie,
Rendus précieux par ces éclairs de la mémoire,
Je vous contemple instants de mes heurs et malheurs,
Trop pauvre que je suis pour dédaigner si peu.

Pell–Mell

A voice that says: "You wanted it this way"
And the same room the next morning.

Another that says: "You shouldn't have"
And its resonance through the years.

A child who says: "I don't know how to love"
An adult listens and doesn't understand.

A soldier who weeps beside a wadi
Another who laughs, dying for nothing.

The letter within plain sight of inquisitive eyes
That told nothing that wasn't already known.

An afternoon of quatorze juillet
The fireworks display below the roofs.

A midnight train for Dieppe and Le Havre
And two innocents dreaming America.

Aspirin eucharist swallowed in haste
And that nausea that never ends.

The enraptured crowd a rapid farewell
A word underlined in the dictionary.

The stairway lonely hearts department
The urging of a gaze one will not see again.

Tarnished under dust and behind dirty glass,
Gilded by the lightning of memory,
I consider you, moments of my happiness and distress,
Being too poor to disdain so little.

L'Heure qu'il est

"Ne descendez pas trop" dit-elle. "En bas
On s'écrase comme punaises sous la semelle.
Sentez-vous la puanteur qui épaissait
Sur la langue le goût de l'air?"
L'homme dardé de flèches défraîchies
Laissa comme un regret le bord de l'abîme de boue.
Il avait tant rêvé d'aller voir comment grouillent
Les cohortes semblables à ses fantasmes
Qui copulent au plis de ses nuits
Se reproduisent en progression érotique
Et finissent par s'endormir
Repus d'abjection satisfaite
Prêts à crever pour prix de leurs délices.

"N'insistez pas" dit-elle. "Il sera temps
Quand leur petite machine programmée pour ces exploits
Cessera sa course sur les parois de l'égout
Quand l'air méphitique se fera rare à leurs poumons
D'aller noter sur les faces à l'agonie
Quels interdits ils ont enfreints quelle
Facette de la nuit ils n'ont pas su
Distinguer dans leur frénésie quel
Monstre ils n'ont pas vu que cachait le temps."
L'homme bardé d'impatience irraisonnée
Se laissa glisser lentement vers l'abîme
L'oeil fixé sur sa montre. "Il est l'heure" dit-il
"De connaître par moi-même ce qu'est la vie."

What Time It Is

"Don't go down too far," she said, "Down there
They're getting crushed like bedbugs under someone's shoes
Don't you smell the stench that thickens
The taste of the air on your tongue?"
The man pierced with shopworn arrows
Left behind like a regret the brink of the abyss of mud.
He had been so eager to see the swarming
Of cohorts that might have resembled his phantasms,
That copulate in the folds of nights
Reproduce in an erotic progression,
And end by falling asleep
Glutted with abject satisfactions,
Ready to burst as the price of their delectations.

"Don't insist," she said. "There will be time
Enough when their little machine, programmed for these exploits,
Will cease to run around the brim of the sewer,
When the mephitic air will grow thin in their lungs,
To go and observe the death-agony on their faces—
What interdicts they infringed what
Facet of the night they weren't able
To distinguish in their frenzy what
Monsters hidden by time they failed to see."
The man encased in unreasonable impatience
Let himself slide slowly toward the abyss,
His eye fixed on his watch. "It's time," he said,
"To go see for myself what life is."

Une Veuve

Des fontaines s'allumaient sous nos pas ce soir-là
Des colonnes supportaient les châteaux inaccessibles
Ce soir-là. Le ciel mauve illuminait d'orages
Devant des mille-fleurs les vénéneux cattleyas.

Comment va-t-on au pied des tours jumelles?
On n'y va pas. Les tours ont étouffé les rues.
Rien ne conduit alors au fleuve sous ses ponts?
Une ville reconnue nous rapproche d'hier.

Devant un lion de pierre au blason émoussé
Debout, était-ce moi? Mon ombre à ses genoux pliée
Etait-ce lui? La fenêtre donnait sur la gare
Le néon balbutiait un temps semblable au temps.

Enfin réconciliés entre bonsoir et baiser
Entre hier et demain qui suspend l'insomnie
Nous avons découvert notre première nuit
Oubliant le regret des chambres séparées.

Comment va-t-on aux douves feuillues aux remparts?
On n'y va plus. Les tours rasées ont comblé le fossé
Un adieu s'est noué au fil des voies ferrées
Le jour a retrouvé ses contours oubliés.

Dans un désert d'obstacles et d'objets désolés
Vivante était-ce moi clouée à la trace de rêves
Pleurant ces mains nouées qu'un départ a tranchées
Moi qu'alourdit le deuil d'un bonheur oublié?

A Widow

Fountains came alight under our feet that evening
Columns supported inaccessible castles
That evening. The violet sky lit storms
Of blossoming fireworks behind the poisonous cattleyas.

How does one get to the foot of the twin towers?
One doesn't. The towers have stifled the streets.
Then nothing leads to the river under the bridges?
A recognized city reproaches us with yesterday.

In front of a stone lion with a mossy coat-of-arms
Was it me, standing? My shadow bent at his knees
Was it him? The window gave on the station
The neon stammered a weather that was like the weather.

Reconciled at last between goodnight and kisses
Between yesterday and tomorrow which defers insomnia
We discovered our first night
Forgetting the regret of separate bedrooms.

How does one get to the leafy moats at the ramparts?
One doesn't anymore. The razed towers have filled the ditch
A farewell tied itself to the wire of the railway
Day rediscovered its forgotten contours.

In a desert of obstacles and desolate objects
Was it me alive nailed to the trace of dreams
Weeping for my bound hands that a departure has cut off
Me weighted with mourning a forgotten happiness?

Rien à dire

Porte ouverte sur rien à dire
Chambre réelle clair tombeau
Je meurs je vis murs éclatés éblouissante
Lumière cours fracassant du temps
L'histoire s'attache à mes membres
Je vis je rêve entre ses rives
Gravées d'innombrables annales
Autre tombe d'éternité
Table de bronze où l'on dissèque
Parmi les idées écaillées
Mon corps irradiant ses folies
Au front fêlé d'un dieu qui ne se connaît pas
Et qui pourtant devrait connaître
Pourquoi cette porte est béante
Pourquoi la chambre ouverte donne
Sur le tombeau sur rien à dire.

Nothing to Say

Door open on nothing to say
Actual bedroom daylit tomb
I die I live burst walls blinding
Light splintering flow of time
History sticks to my limbs
I live I dream between its banks
Graven with innumerable annals
Another tomb of eternity
Bronze table where they dissect
Among flaking ideas
My body radiating its madness
To the cracked forehead of a god
Who doesn't recognize himself
But who still ought to know why
This door is gaping
Why the open bedroom gives on
The tomb, on nothing to say.

Trois Petits Poèmes

I

Un pays différent du nôtre
meurt sur les doigts d'un
feu de bois. Le ciel se
couche alors sur moi et le
soleil me prend la bouche.

Contrée, tes arbres sont
entrés l'un dans l'autre
et nos mains jointes créent
un royaume où se perdre est
se retrouver.

II

Aux attaches des plus précieuses
parures stagne le temps qui garde
toute moiteur jusqu'à ce que ton
corps y nage remontant ses propres
rigueurs.
        Les eaux premières à la
source composent selon le nouvel
ordre et le prochain reflet un
cours dont les méandres touchent
tout instant pour mieux l'émouvoir

Ainsi s'étale un lit que le ciel
ignorait où gisent le fugace et
l'instable dans le cheminement de
rares géographies.

Three Little Poems

I

A country different from ours
dies on   the fingers of a
wood fire.   The sky then
sets   on   me   and   the
sun   takes   my   mouth.

Land,   your   trees   have
entered   one   another
and our joined hands create
a kingdom where being lost
is being found.

II

At the clasp of the most precious
sets of jewelry stagnates the climate that
keeps   all   its   .clamminess   until   your
body swims upstream against its own
rigors.
    The   first   waters   at   the
spring   compose   according   to   the
new   rule   and   the   next   reflection
a   stream   whose   meanders   touch
each   instant   the   better   to   excite   it

Thus   a   bed   sprawls   that   the   sun
didn't know about, wherein lie the fleeting
and   the   unstable   in   the   advancing   of
rare geographies.

III

Nuit réduite à la ligne nue où
se joignent les paupières quand
la lampe et son jour faux cessent
de meurtrir nos yeux.

Derrière
tu vois l'écran des apparences
conservées les modulations du
néant l'échappatoire inconsciente.

III

Night reduced to the naked line where
The   eyelids   join   when
the lamp and its false daylight cease
to bruise our eyes.

                          Behind
you   see   the   screen   of   kept-up
appearances   the   modulations   of
nothingness the unconscious loophole.

Toten Insel

La voix connue, un vieil ami m'arrache aux délices du port
Et tandis que nous remontons ensemble vers le bois de myrtes:
"Dis-moi," dit-il, prenant ma main comme au temps de nos promenades,
"Pourquoi tu arrives déjà et comment tu fis le chemin.
À cette heure-ci les bureaux sont fermés . . .
On peut d'ailleurs attendre aussi longtemps qu'on veut avant d'entrer . . .
Impossible de se perdre, inutile de s'inquiéter.
On peut aussi se promener si on le désire
Aussi longtemps qu'on le désire."

Et moi, me retournant, je ne vois plus rien sur l'autre bord
Qu'un pan doré de brumes, qu'îles avec des photographies reflétées,
Et les mâtures, les bateaux, les branches d'arbres calcinées,
Quelque chose comme un adieu figé entre le ciel et l'eau.

C'est pire que prévu mais le pire était prévu.

Si encore, j'étais sûr
D'être ici
De vous avoir retrouvés
De parler
Et d'éprouver avec vous
Des regrets . . .

Les maisons se ressemblent toutes
Des fleurs séchées parmi le sable des allées.
D'une terrasse à l'autre un téléphone permettrait . . .
Mais est-ce bien la même maison et n'y a-t-il pas
D'océan entre les îles rendant toute conversation impossible
Parce qu'il pleut? Surtout que . . . parlons nous vraiment la même
        langue?

Toten Insel*

The familiar voice, an old friend plucks me from the harbor's delights
And as we climb together toward the myrtle wood:
"Tell me," he says, taking my hand as in the time of our excursions,
"Why you arrive so soon, and how you journeyed.
At this hour the offices are closed . . .
Besides, you can wait as long as you like without going in . . .
It's impossible to get lost, and pointless to worry.
Or we can go for a walk, if you wish,
For as long as you wish."

And turning, I no longer see anything on the other shore,
Nothing but a gilded patch of fog, islands, with reflected photographs,
And the masts and spars, the boats, the charred branches of trees,
Something like a goodbye frozen between the sky and the water.

It's worse than predicted, but the worst was predicted.

Yet if only I was sure
Of being here,
Of having found you all again
Of speaking
And of feeling regret
With you . . .

The houses all look alike:
Dried flowers along the sandy walks.
From one terrace to another a telephone would allow . . .
But is this really the same house and isn't there
Ocean among the islands making all conversation impossible
Because it's raining? Especially since . . . are we really speaking the same
       language?

*The Isle of the Dead, the title of an Arnold Böcklin painting which inspired this
poem. (Trans.)

J'ai commencé à perdre espoir un soir
Lorsque cherchant encore à croire à une aurore
Je savais que le jour glisserait hors de la nuit
Sans moi,
Effleurant les arbres les antennes les corniches
Et toucherait, à travers la vitre, mon visage
Couvert, ayant accepté le poids du drap, moi qui
À la moindre main près de mon sommeil m'éveillais.
C'était donc l'aube où je devrais naître à jamais,
Que j'avais tant redoutée, m'attendant
À des convulsions des éclats de sanie sur les murs
À des horreurs hurlées.
Mais:
J'étais seulement debout devant un magasin d'autographes.
Sous une vitre, une lettre dont mon reflet cachait les lignes
Adressée à moi était à vendre. Et j'ai glissé
Sur le trottoir comme une serviette mouillée ...
Ou bien
J'écoutais après un court dîner après l'amour,
L'autre à peine parti, son odeur à mes doigts,
Mon coeur ralentir tout à coup puis sursauter
Et se taire ...
Ou bien
J'entrais en un rêve et croyais y courir
Après un enfant nu que cachaient les buissons
Et qui, passant à gué une rivière,
Tout emperlé de gouttelettes d'arc-en-ciel
De la rive adverse en chantant exaltait
La tiédeur de sa main le chaud de son aisselle
Le velours de son flanc ou ses armes.
Et j'étouffais en me noyant dans les rapides ...

J'avais appris la joie, la vie, parmi de jeunes fous,
Colibris colorés dansant autour de moi.
Dans un jardin pailleté, sous des arches en feuillées,

I began to lose hope one evening
When, still trying to believe in a dawn,
I knew that day would slide out of night
                    Without me,
Grazing the trees the antennas the cornices
And would touch, through the pane, my covered
Face, which had accepted the weight of the sheet, I who
Used to waken at the slightest hand near my sleep.
So it was the dawn when I was to be born forever,
That I had dreaded so much, expecting
Convulsions, shards of pus on the walls,
Shouted horrors.
                    But:
I was only standing in front of an autograph shop.
Under glass, where my reflection hid the lines,
A letter addressed to me was for sale,
And I slipped on the sidewalk like a wet towel . . .
                    Or else
I was listening—after a brief dinner, after love,
The other had barely left, his smell still on my fingers—
To my heart slacken all at once, then start
And fall silent . . .
                    Or else
I was entering a dream where I thought I ran
After a naked child screened by bushes
Who, fording a river,
Beaded with rainbow drops,
Singing from the opposite bank, intensified
The warmth of his hand, the heat of his armpit,
The down of his side or his weapons.
And I choked, drowning in the rapids . . .

I had learned joy, life, among young madmen,
Colored hummingbirds dancing around me.
In a spangled garden, under leafy arches,

Une licorne assise aux feux des cheminées
Pâle, lustrait sa croupe, seins dardés,
Platon ouvert devant des carafes vidées
Et sur le mur une ombre une horloge figée
Moi qui entre, moi qui refuse de me perdre
Parmi toutes délices escomptées.

Cherchais-je une fontaine ou bien l'oubli
Un astrolabe ou l'équipage d'un galion
Pour boire avec moi à ma soif?
Des pigeons polluaient l'eau du lac
À moins que ce ne fût une ombelle tombée
À moins que ce ne fussent phrases mal réglées:
"Nos bicyclettes renversées sur les zinnias . . ."
Où allais-je sans autre carte qu'un miroir?
Chaque visage au soir jaillissait du cambouis
Comme une insulte à un appareil génital
Et les yeux regardaient qui les regarde
Vaciller, tenir à distance, tandis que
La beauté battait le tambour aux fenêtres:
Chambres scellées personne pour crier au feu!
Alors je vis passer quelqu'un au pied du lit
Sans savoir si c'était moi ou personne.
La lampe brillait sans courant.
Le dos des livres parlait une langue indécise
Les bruits de la rue ne rapprochaient plus les charrois familiers.
Je prenais une main qui ne palpitait plus.
Je sifflais, et des voix frileuses emmitouflées
Ne répondaient pas à leur nom pourtant hurlé
Comme si elles étaient sourdes.
Ou mortes.

Je tourne autour du silence.
Le puits sans profondeur n'a plus d'eau pour ma soif.
Là je m'abîme, néant discret,

A unicorn seated by the fires of fireplaces,
Pale, polished its flank, its breasts pointed,
Plato open before the emptied flasks
And on the wall a shadow a congealed clock
Me going in, me who refuses to lose me
Among all anticipated pleasures.

Was I looking for a fountain or was it oblivion
An astrolabe or the crew of a galleon
To drink with me to my thirst?
Pigeons polluted the lake water
Unless it was a fallen umbel,
Unless it was badly-worded phrases:
"Our bicycles overturned on the zinnias . . ."
Where was I going with no other map than a mirror?
At evening each face shot up out of the motor oil
Like an insult to a genital organ
And the eyes looked at who watches them
Vacillate, keeping a distance, while
Beauty beat the drum at the windows:
The rooms sealed, no one to cry "Fire!"
Then I saw someone pass the foot of the bed,
Not knowing if it was myself or no one.
The lamp glowed without electric current.
The spines of books spoke an imprecise language,
The sounds of the street no longer brought the familiar carts closer.
I pressed a hand that no longer palpitated.
I whistled, and chilly muffled voices
Didn't answer to their name, though it was shouted.
As though they were deaf.
Or dead.

I hang around silence.
The depthless well has no more water for my thirst.
There I am swallowed up, discreet nothingness,

Là où imperceptiblement m'a conduit ma vie.
Là je tombe
Ayant toujours ignoré tout pourquoi.
Mais les jours et les nuits de ma quête,
Qui les a contemplés, témoin glacé, sans voir
Qu'une flamme dormait au tréfonds de mon sang?
Les livres lus de compagnie
Les musiques et les musées
Les paysages habités
M'auront laissé seul.
Et le ciel même où je ne retrouve pas
La couleur durable du temps
Tourne n'importe comment, toutes étoiles brouillées,
Si confusément que je crois marcher droit
Dans un monde aux itinéraires fermés,
Sang sur lui-même bouclé
Cercle des méridiens sans fin.
Si peu de jours rattrapant le temps donné . . .
Et si peu de mots répétés par tant de bouches
Maintenant que je commence à n'être rien.

"Inutile de s'inquiéter
Impossible de se perdre
On peut toujours se promener si on le désire
Aussi longtemps qu'on le désire . . ."

This poem and translation first appeared in *Every Question but One*. (Eds.)

There where my life has imperceptibly led me.
There, I fall
Having never known any why.
But the days and nights of my search,
Who has gazed on them, a frozen witness, without seeing
That a flame slept in the deepest strata of my blood?
The books read in company,
The musics and museums
The inhabited landscapes
Will have left me alone.
And even the sky, where I no longer find
The lasting color of the weather,
Turns every which way, all stars scrambled,
So vaguely that I think I'm walking straight
In a world of closed circuits,
Blood coiled on itself
Encircles endless meridians.
So few days overtaking the time that is given . . .
And so few words repeated by so many mouths
Now that I'm beginning to be nothing.

"It's pointless to worry
Impossible to get lost,
Or we can go for a walk if you wish,
For as long as you wish . . ."

Toutes les questions sauf une

Le public est libre de poser
Toutes les questions
      Sauf une
Sous peine de disparaître
      Dans la trappe
Ouverte par le meneur de jeu
      Un homme gras
Masqué de papier journal enflammé.

Je puis commencer ma prière in petto
Et finir par recevoir
Un morceau de sucre sur la langue
Pour arriver—dans quel état—
À la tranche des galaxies
Nuit de quatorze juillet pleine de gloire
      Et découvrir
Qu'il y a d'autres découvertes à faire.

L'étincelle d'absence
Contenue dans le temps
Le chemin à l'envers
Vers l'explosion originelle
Et derrière l'homme au masque
Quelle imposture voilée
Elle aussi pour interdire
De savoir quoi demander ?
      A qui?

Il faudrait recommencer la séance
Avec d'autres spectateurs
Briser toutes les idoles
Sans en dresser de nouvelles

Every Question but One

The audience is free to ask
Every question
      But one
On pain of disappearing
      Through the trapdoor
Opened by the master of ceremonies
      A heavy man
Masked with flaming newsprint.

I can start my prayer *in petto*
And end by receiving
A lump of sugar on my tongue
To arrive—but in what condition!—
At the cut edge of the galaxies
The night of July fourteenth full of glory
      And discover
That there are other discoveries to make.

The spark of absence
Contained in time
The road backward
Toward the original explosion
And behind the man with the mask
What veiled trickery
Is also there to forbid
Knowing what to ask for?
      Of whom?

We would have to start the performance again
With other spectators
Smash all the idols
Without erecting new ones

Et si nous trouvons l'être au masque
Celui qui n'existe pas
Transgresser nos angoisses
Et lui casser la gueule.
       Peut-être . . .

This poem and translation first appeared in *Every Question but One*. (Eds.)

And if we find the creature with the mask
The one who doesn't exist
Disobey our anxieties
And smash his face.
        Perhaps. . . .

Passant la frontière

La ligne se voyait depuis
Longtemps au gré de la route
Et si l'on s'endormait au volant
Fulgurait dans l'âme assoupie
Comme une révélation brutale
Qui vous évitait de sentir
Dans l'instantané onirique
Votre cervelle s'écraser
Sur la borne ou le pare-brise

C'était une ligne idéale
Sommée de bleu horizontal
Qui déployait jour aprés jour
Comme la corde d'une lessive
Drapeaux et scalps et roses délavés
Nos pays nos combats nos guerres
Mêlant lassitude et sursauts
Une gymnastique en désordre
Qui rendait malade nos coeurs

Passing the Frontier

The yellow line could be seen for as long a time
As the highway desired
And if you fell asleep at the wheel
It fulgurated in the dozing soul
Like a brutal revelation
That allows you not to feel
In the dream's snapshot
Your brain getting smashed
Against the milestone or the windshield

It was an ideal line
Crowned with horizontal blue
That unwound day after day
Like a clothesline
Flags and scalps and washed-out roses
Our countries our combats our wars
Mingling lassitude with involuntary starts
A gymnastic in disorder
That sickened our hearts

Ganymède

Un mur, un miroir: c'est le ciel, n'est-ce pas?

Par les éclats du jour entre l'hélicoptère.
Il enlève dans ses serres un clerc endormi,
L'emporte par des corridors aseptisés
Jusqu'à l'Olympe où règne—parmi l'acier,
Les horoscopes, les hormones, les ordures—
Vieille première communiante violée,
La Ville, enrubannée de méphitiques nuées.

C'est ici, enfin, que tout s'explique:

"...Je viens d'une ferme où le tabac croît
Sous un velum impénétrable aux bactéries ...
Là, dans un hallier touffu de feuilles molles
Que sur sa cuisse nue une nymphe écrasait,
J'ai grandi, par moi-même à moi-même enchaîné ..."

"...Une yole fendait le lac un jour de pluie,
Tirée par de gros gars oints de suif, leurs mains
Cousues pour écarter les tentations,
Jusqu'à la rive adverse empoisonnée de lierre ..."

"...J'ai lu la Bible entre des herbes stupéfiantes
Et saint François dans un bol de lait bleu ..."

"...J'ai voulu mourir à bicyclette mais midi
N'a pas duré assez longtemps pour me percer ..."

"...Un matin traversé d'orages magnétiques,
Le ventre creux, j'ai monté, descendu sans fin
Un escalier glacé au flanc d'un gâteau d'anges ..."

Ganymede

A wall, a mirror: it's the sky, isn't it?

Through the shards of the day the helicopter enters.
It seizes a sleeping clerk in its claws,
Carries him off through antiseptic corridors
To Olympus, where amid steel, horoscopes, hormones,
Garbage, the City—ribboned with mephitic thunderheads:
An old, violated first communicant—rules.

It's here, finally, that everything is explained:

". . . I come from a farm where tobacco grows
Under an awning bacteria cannot penetrate . . .
There in a dense thicket of soft leaves
That a nymph crushed against her naked thigh,
I grew up, chained by myself to myself . . ."

". . . A yawl cleaved the lake one rainy day
Drawn by big guys smeared with suet, their hands
Sewn shut to avoid temptations
As far as the opposite shore, poisoned with ivy . . ."

". . . I read the Bible amid narcotic herbs
And St. Francis in a bowl of blue milk . . ."

". . . I wanted to die on a bicycle but noon
Didn't last long enough to pierce me . . ."

". . . On a morning traversed by electric storms,
On an empty stomach, I climbed, I walked endlessly down
A frozen staircase in the side of an angel's cake . . ."

C'est tout. Le reste a pris plus de temps
À passer qu'à demeurer dans ma mémoire.
Et maintenant, pressé sous le poids du béton
Je sue lentement, par tous les sphincters, l'ennui.
Cela dépend du ciel, des plaisirs collectifs,
De la douleur, des auréoles, des capsules.
Et les rideaux ne prennent plus feu,
Les phénix se sont coupés les empennages,
Les rhododendrons se ratatinent jusqu'au soir,
Dans le parc, près de flaques
Où se reflètent vos mamelles taries
Grande soeur délavée d'indifférence.
Un vague murmure chlorophyllique demeure,
Lointain brouhaha, toutes portes fermées.

Bientôt c'est la nuit. La Grande Ourse d'avril
Entourée d'îles étincelle.
L'acier d'aujourd'hui fulgure et d'acryliques
Toisons emmaillotent les banknotes.

Je me suis dévêtu sur un rythme syncopé—
Tantôt négresse huilée, tantôt blanche hétaïre
Roses noires à l'aisselle et tintamarre au flanc,
Pour réveiller ces bambins pneumatiques
Leur chyle homogénéisé, leurs ridicules.
Ils frappent sur le clavicorde en kit
Construit après les heures de bureau
La monnaie bidon de Jean-Sébastien Bach,
Absorbée, ingérée, digérée, imprimée
En circuits microscopiques sous leurs lobes.
Maintenant le store à peine tiré devant le permanent
Scintillement des journaux lumineux, des phares,
Difficile de les distraire du Zen, des pilules,
Des vacances vendues en culottes bermudiennes,
Un grand rhum au poing, le couchant flamboyant

That's all. The rest took more time to happen
Than to lodge in my memory.
And now, pressed under the weight of concrete
I sweat boredom slowly, through all my sphincters.
That depends on the sky, on collective pleasures,
On pain, haloes, capsules.
And the curtains no longer catch fire,
The phoenixes have shorn their plumage,
The rhododendrons shrink until evening.
In the park, near the puddles
Where your dried-up breasts are reflected—
Big sister washed out by indifference.
A vague chlorophyllic murmur stays,
Distant hubbub, all doors shut.

Soon it will be night. The Great Bear of April
Sparkles, surrounded by islands.
The steel of today fulgurates and acrylic
Fleece swaddles the banknotes.

I undressed to a syncopated rhythm—
Sometimes an oiled negress, sometimes a white whore
Black roses at her armpits and noise at her sides,
To waken those pneumatic urchins,
Their homogenized chyle, their ridicule.
On the clavichord built from a kit
After office hours
They strike the counterfeit coins of Johann Sebastian Bach
—Absorbed, ingested, digested, printed
In microscopic circuits under their lobes.
Now with the shade barely raised to reveal the permanent
Glitter of the flashing news-bulletins, the lighthouses,
It's difficult to distract them from Zen, from pills,
From sold vacations in Bermuda shorts—
A large rum in the fist, the sunset blazing

À contre-jour dans le duvet de leur jarret.
Difficile de les arracher au poison électronique,
Distillé parmi les déchets industriels,
Aux chiens fous entre les autos, qu'on écrase,
À ce mirage ondoyant de lendemains plus beaux.
Nous avons essayé la lutte, la contrainte, et
L'abominable persuasion, mes frères et moi.
La croix séchait au pied de notre lit.
La poussière des révolutions avortées
Donnait plus soif encore aux ivrognes roulant
Dans la fange du réel le rêve des hommes.

C'est alors qu'il fallait réapprendre à tourner
Le bois, à tisser l'écorce, à épier le caribou
Les pieds dans des marais gélatineux, seul,
Appuyé sur la lointaine fumée des crépuscules,
À gâcher la science ancestrale avilie
Et chauler la neuve maison.
C'est alors qu'il fallait remonter
Le plus simple jouet pour chanter des merveilles
Et découvrir dans le creux des jours et des nuits
La chaleur des autres. Et l'aimer.
Mais les épis s'étiolent sous la cendre,
D'arrogants bulldozers déciment nos journées,
Arrachent les dolmens, langue coupée le long de la route,
Et de sombres idiots fouillent les tas de feuilles
Mortes sans inventer, sans deviner, sans même voir
L'étincelle sur quoi il suffirait de souffler.
Et quand ils auront fui les moustiques et les herbes,
De grands Indiens, leur pénis peint, leur oeil cerné,
Violeront dans un mirage d'obsidienne
Leurs filles, leurs chevaux et leur rêve d'Indiens.
On retourne à l'histoire racontée aux enfants
Par ces grands loups gris comme n'est plus leur pain.
Les enfants vont encore à l'école aujourd'hui; leur voix,
Orange trop mûre, tombe en plis au pied du drapeau.

From behind on the down of their shanks.
It's hard to tear them from the electronic poison
Distilled amid industrial waste,
From the mad dogs squashed between the cars,
From this wavy mirage of lovelier tomorrows.
We tried struggle, constraint, and
Abominable persuasion, my brothers and I.
The cross dried up at the foot of our bed.
The dust of aborted revolutions
Made the drunks still thirstier as they rolled
The dream of men in the muck of reality.

It's then that we should have learned again to turn
Wood, weave bark, watch for caribou,
Feet in the gelatinous marshes, alone,
Leaning on the distant smoke of twilights,
To spoil the debased ancestral knowledge,
To lime the new house.
It's then we should wind up
The simplest toy to sing of marvels
And discover in the hollows of the days and nights
The heat of others. And to love it.
But the ears of wheat wilt under ash,
Arrogant bulldozers decimate our days,
Rip up the dolmens, tongue cut all along the highways,
And somber idiots burrow in piles of dead leaves
Without inventing, without guessing, without even seeing
The spark on which it would suffice to blow.
And when they will have fled the mosquitoes and the weeds,
Tall Indians with painted penises and rings under their eyes
Will rape in an obsidian mirage
Their daughters, their horses, and their dream of Indians.
We go back to history as it's told to children
By great gray wolves, gray as their bread no longer is.
The children still go to school even today; their voices,
A too-ripe orange, fall in folds at the base of the flag.

Vive les villes verticales
Les piscines au haut des tours
Défi aux hordes de vandales
Durs symboles de faux amours!
Vive les vertes ice-cream
Tournant au rose sous la langue,
Les TV et les limousines,
Les diaphragmes et les amants
Perdus dans les champs d'épandage
Les oiseleurs les assassins
Gravant leur nom dans les écorces
Leur ombre en polaroïd!

Olympus, putain chevelue
Dont le nombril électrifié
Suinte d'encre et les paupières
S'alourdissent de bismuth
Quand les chats pissent dans les caves
Quand les soldats quittent Beyrouth
Quand les geishas percent leur ventre
Quand les pompiers glissent le long
De perches chromées sexe en mains.
C'est moi qui connais la musique
C'est moi qui écris aux journaux
Qui crie le prix du lait, qui rase
Les jambes paires des Rockettes
C'est moi qui ajoute des ailes
Aux chiens poursuivant l'oncle Tom
Et applaudis aux étincelles
Qui lancent vers la Lune l'homme
Rivé à la chaise électrique!

Lequel de vous est vraiment Jupiter?

Long live vertical cities
Swimming pools on the tops of towers
Challenge to the hordes of vandals
Hard symbols of fake loves!
Long live green ice cream
Turning pink under the tongue,
TV's and limousines
Diaphragms, lovers,
Lost in the sewage farms
Bird catchers and murderers
Carving their names in bark
Their shadows in polaroid!

Mount Olympus great hairy whore
Whose electrified navel
Oozes ink and whose eyelids
Grow heavy with bismuth
When cats are pissing in cellars
When the soldiers leave Beirut
When geishas pierce their bellies
When firemen slide down the long
Nickel-plated pole prick in hand.
It's I who knows the music
It's I who writes to the newspapers
Who shouts the price of milk, who shaves
The even-numbered legs of Rockettes
It's I who adds wings
To the dogs set on Uncle Tom
And applauds the sparks that send
Moonward the man
Riveted to the electric chair!

Which one of you is really Jupiter?

Une Nuit sur la mer Morte

Toute chambre est vide
Tout parfum évanoui
Toute présence absente.

Un rideau sépare l'aube
Palme peinte oiseaux silencieux
De la froide nuit intérieure.

L'hôtel éteint s'envole vers
Quelque Far-West onirique
Où le cheval monte l'Indien

Où le sable roux des falaises
Se fige en une statue comme
À Sodome la femme de Loth.

Le soleil transparent dessine
Sur la peau sur le sel séché
Des cristaux joyaux improbables

À offir à celle qui chante
Aux rives bitumeuses la
Saison heureuse le sommeil.

A Night on the Dead Sea

Every bedroom is empty
Every perfume vanished
Every presence absent.

A curtain screens the dawn
Painted palm silent birds
From the cold night inside.

The extinct hotel flies away
Toward some oneiric Far West
Where the horse mounts the Indian

Where the reddish sand of the cliffs
Congeals into a statue
Like Lot's wife in Sodom.

The transparent sun traces
On the skin on the dried salt
Crystals improbable jewels

To offer to her
On the bituminous banks,
Who sings of sleep, the fortunate season.

Le Paysagiste

Le grand calme de la mer et des cieux,
L'effroi né des vagues et des nuages—
Miroirs se reflétant eux-mêmes—
Où tourner le regard?
                              Vaut-il mieux
Fermer les yeux et s'absorber
Dans la rumeur intérieure qui refuse
De voir pour mieux faire?
                              Les yeux fermés, donc!
En bas, au ras des flots, montagnes et vallées
Se bousculent et leur double lointain
Limite l'étendue, l'espace, la distance
Sans comparaison possible, sinon là-haut,
Plus mobile écran du soleil, l'errance des nuées.
Les étoiles s'allument sur le noir infini
Trop connu.
                    Le tableau de la nuit
Ne laisse pas de place pour un rêve.
Attendons la véritable nuit.
                              La profondeur
Des yeux clos révèle l'univers en ses abîmes.
À la surface, une prairie enluminée, vert-bleuté
Sans nuance, reçoit, comme une cascade raidie
D'eau vivifiante, les rayons du vrai jour:
Coulée de temps, un peu dure, laser solidifié.
Qu'il faut briser, découper, renvoyer sur elle-même,
Feux de saphir sur feux d'émeraude
Taillant en mille facettes le ciel reflété.
Alors
            abstrait de l'ébloui
                              est tracé
                                          un arbre.

The Landscapist

The great calm of the sea and the skies
The fear born of waves and clouds—
Mirrors reflecting themselves—
Where should we look?
                         Is it better
To shut one's eyes and absorb
Yourself in the inner noise which refuses
To see in order to do better?
                         Eyes shut, then!
Down there, level with the waves, both mountains and valleys
Elbow each other and their far-off replicas
Limit the expanse, the space, the distance
With no possible comparison, unless up there,
More mobile screen of the sun, the odyssey of clouds.
The stars come alight against the too well-known
Infinite dark.
                 The picture of night
Leaves no place for a dream.
Let's wait for the real night.
                         The depth
Of closed eyes reveals the universe in its chasms.
On its surface, an illuminated meadow, matte bluish green,
Receives, like a rigid waterfall
Of vivifying water, rays of the true day:
Time's flow, somewhat hard, solidified laser.
That must be cut up, broken, thrown back on itself,
Flashes of sapphire on emerald flares,
Cutting the reflected sky into a thousand facets.
Then
          abstracted from the dazzle
                         a tree
                                   is traced.

Ce n'est pas un dessin appliqué
Comme celui qui aurait abouti à un brin d'herbe
Courbe harmonieuse sous le poids de la lumière
Si semblable dans son essence, quoiqu'incomparablement
Unique à d'autres brins, peints avec autant d'attention.
Le temps passe. Les ombres tournent,
La surface veloutée obscure peu à peu se peuple
D'une myriade—pour peu qu'on les observe à l'échelle requise—
De vies distinctes, mobiles malgré leurs racines,
Éparses dans les ténèbres, sans témoin,
Mais vibrant, épelant de leur miroitement de moire
Une tension hors du vert et du bleu.

Et l'arbre, né de la main, tache panache,
Accident?
                    L'arbre échappe à tout concept.
Le désordre réglé de ses branches n'obéit à aucun
Rythme. On passerait des siècles à figurer
Une raison à l'imagination qu'il proclame.
Sa liberté ne peut être qu'un absolu,
Enfermée qu'elle est dans des lois qui
Dépassent toute idée de loi.
                    Pourquoi ces branches,
Ces bouquets, ce brouillard de feuilles, paroles du vent,
Cette broussaille de brindilles, balancée par l'hiver,
Qui avec la saison, reviendront plus touffues, plus hautes,
Et vertes, aussi longtemps que le bleu du ciel le permet?
Pour le savoir, faire un autre arbre,
Sur le même plan fou, dans toutes ses dimensions
Posant—toujours multipliée—la même énigme.
Puis d'autres, au lointain ou plus près,
Étagés de plein ou de vide selon
Les distributions dans l'espace,
Entre lesquels le regard s'insinuera comme les pas
D'une promenade. Où la lumière et les ombres

It's not an applied design
Like the one that would have ended in a blade of grass
Harmonious in its bending under the weight of the light
So similar in essence and yet incomparably
Unique next to other blades, painted with the same attention.
Time passes. The shadows turn,
The dark velvet surface is gradually peopled with millions—
If one but takes the trouble to view them in perspective—
Of distinct lives, mobile despite their roots,
Sparse in the shadows, without witnesses
But vibrant, spelling out with their sheen of watered silk
A tension beyond green and blue.

And the tree, born of the hand, tufted stain?
An accident?
                    The tree eluded every concept.
The regulated disorder of its branches obeys no
Rhythm. One could spend centuries trying to deduce
A reason for the imagination it announces.
Its liberty can only be absolute,
Enclosed, as it is, in the laws which surpass
Every idea of law.
                    Why these branches,
These bouquets, this fog of leaves, words of the wind,
This undergrowth of twigs swept away by winter,
That will return with the season, thicker, taller,
And green, as long as the blue of the sky allows it?
To know this, make another tree,
On the same mad scale in all its dimensions
Proposing the same enigma always multiplied.
Then others in the distance or closer,
Terraced in fullness or emptiness according to
Their distribution in space,
Among which the gaze insinuates itself as the steps
Of a stroll might. Where the light and the shadow

Portées par les choses s'allumeront et s'en iront
Tournant autour d'un axe. Où le monde
Sera tangible, sera chaud et froid,
Imprégné d'air invisible comme l'eau dans une éponge.
Qu'importe alors l'océan sans nom, le ciel
Sans doute inhabité, sinon d'astres problématiques,
Le pourquoi des prairies, de l'herbe dessinée
Au pied de l'arbre. Et l'arbre lui-même!
Que l'esprit s'ouvre aux évidences palpables,
Chaque curiosité autour de chaque chose enroulée,
Chaque désir satisfait d'être réalisable—peut-être—
Quelque part ailleurs que sous l'écrasant infini,
Toutes les fantaisies possibles, lacs, rochers,
Variété innombrable de verdures, changeant avec le temps,
Qu'il faudra dénombrer, qualifier avec autant
De nuances qu'elle en comporte, et peupler—
Alors que l'oeil dissipe la taie qui lui cache
Les hautes herbes sur les pentes près du fleuve,
Les algues au profond des eaux, les palmes et les fleurs—
De légions de serpents, d'escadrilles d'oiseaux.

Cast by things will kindle and disappear turning around an axis
Where the world will be tangible and hot and cold,
Impregnated with invisible air like the water in a sponge.
What do they matter then, the nameless ocean and the sky,
Uninhabited, no doubt, except for problematic stars,
The why of the meadows, of the grass drawn
At the foot of the tree. And the tree itself!
You need only open your mind to the palpable
Evidence, each curiosity wrapped around each thing,
Each desire content to be realizable—perhaps—
Somewhere else than under crushing infinity
All the possible fantasies, lakes, cliffs,
Innumerable variety of verdure changing with the weather
Which will have to be counted, qualified with as many nuances
As they contain, and populated—
While the eye disperses the film that hides
The tall grasses on the slopes near the river,
The algae in the depths of the waters, the palms and the flowers—
With legions of serpents, with squadrons of birds.

Des Nuits et des corps

1

Le vent souffle sur mon écharpe ce soir
Comme la terre coule autour des oliviers
Une grande épée flamboie à contre-jour
Une pluie de lumière lavant les eucalyptus.

La voiture domine les falaises urbaines
Quand la nuit fait rentrer dans notre gorge le sang.
O ange qui déploie ses ailes hors de ses jeans
Tes mains sentent la truffe et le vin noir.

Les bouches cherchent leur profondeur secrète.
Le fumet des corps tendus bute sur la vitre
Les yeux se ferment sur une longue attente humide

Et notre vie chargée comme une caméra . . .

2

Je m'habillais pour une visite exemplaire
Et quittais, le corps parfumé, l'air de la chambre.
Le ciel noir, les cloches de tous les jours fêlées,
Pas un lampion ne restait allumé sur la place.

Comme un chat frôlant des papiers usés volant au vent
Le froid poudrait la rue de cristaux et de larmes.
La porte refermée la ville était à moi
L'espoir satinait l'eau vers l'absente Amérique.

Je portais, le long de rails qu'huilait la nuit,
Mon sang, fardeau vivant, et l'offrais à des lèvres
Tapies dans les buissons attendant le hasard
Pour s'ouvrir à cette vraie chaleur du monde.

Of Nights and Bodies

1

The wind blows on my scarf tonight
As earth flows around the olive trees
A big sword flashes against the light
A rain of light washing the eucalyptuses.

My car overlooks urban cliffs
When night puts the blood back in our throats.
O angel unfolding your wings out of your jeans
Your hands smell of truffles and black wine.

The mouths are searching their secret depth
The odor of stiffened bodies knocks against the car window
The eyes are closing on a long damp expectation

And our life is loaded like a camera . . .

2

I was getting dressed for an exemplary visit
And left, body perfumed, the air of the room.
Sky black, everyday bells sounding cracked,
Not a lantern still on in the square.

Like a cat rubbing against soiled papers lifted by the wind
The cold sprinkled the street with crystals and tears.
The door closed behind me the city was mine
Hope made the water satiny toward absent America.

I was carrying my blood along railways oiled by night
Like a living burden, and offered it to lips
Lurking in the bushes waiting for chance
To open themselves to that real warmth of the world.

3

Je raconte souvent à des inconnus dans la nuit
Une vie qui serait la mienne si j'étais un autre
Si j'avais pris d'autres chemins, si, par exemple,
J'avais refusé de garder dans ma main longuement

Le sang d'inconnus dans la nuit comme aujourd'hui.

Je déroule, baignant dans les lumières d'un faux passé
Paysages et visages, accidents et bonheurs,
Pour plaire à qui m'écoute et avec lui peut-être
Exorciser le temps.

Or, toutes ces histoires
Ont l'unique parfum qui fait lever les mêmes
Rêves—éclairs oubliés, mémoires en délire,
Enfances lentes à nourrir autre que moi.

4

Dans combien de miroirs as-tu pris cette image
Mon ange, déguisé en complice? Qui t'a
Fourni l'explication de mes faiblesses?
Empruntes-tu mon sang pour mentir, ou prier?

Ma main, tu la voulais prompte à toutes caresses
Et mon corps tant mêlé à mon coeur dans nos lits
Que je ne sais plus qui de toi ou moi est moi
Innombrable animal que ma peur justifie.

Je te guette au sortir de sommeils sans témoin
Je te traîne dans les décharges de mes jours
Je te cloue aux cloisons dont demain m'environne
Je veux te garder vif en moi jusqu'à ma mort.

3

At night I often tell strangers the story
Of a life that would be mine if I were somebody else
If I had taken other roads, if, for example,
I had refused to keep for long in my hand

The blood of unknown people in the night like today.

Bathing in the lights of a false past I unroll
Landscapes and faces, accidents and good fortune
To please the one who listens to me, and with him perhaps
To exorcise time.

Now, all these stories
Have the single perfume which is raising
The same dreams—forgotten lightning flashes, delirious memories,
Childhoods slow to nourish someone other than me.

4

In how many mirrors have you taken that picture
My angel disguised as an accomplice? Who has
Given you the explanation of my failings?
Are you borrowing my blood for a lie or a prayer?

You wanted my hand ready for every caress
And my body so mixed with my heart in our beds
That I don't know anymore who of you or me is I
Innumerable animal that my fear justifies.

I watch you coming out of sleeps without witnesses
I drag you in the dumping grounds of my days
I nail you to the partitions that tomorrow surrounds me with
I want to keep you alive in me until my death.

5

Découvre-moi comme un paysage par l'aube,
Retiens encore la nuit en ses ombres et laisse
Ton sang dans le matin révéler ses éclats.
Moi, j'atterris,—patience et passion butinées—
Dans l'éden ou l'enfer où je rêvais de toi,
Enrichissant de musc tes cheveux, et de lait
Ton corps, ma galaxie, mes lunes, mon soleil.

Le plaisir est un fleuve intemporel, ses rives
S'écroulent pour mêler les roches et les eaux.
Le coeur y perd son rythme et les mondes tournoient
Recréant le chaos initial où reposent
Nos têtes en explosion éternelle, mon tout . . .

6

Notre histoire a pu commencer dans l'hypothèse
D'un singe primordial aux rotules raidies
Contemplant par-delà les savanes brûlées
La derniére nuée qui blanchit l'horizon.
Il sent vibrer en son crâne un cristal où coule
La mesure du temps, la distance, son sang,
Le sable de ses jours et la désespérance
Les ossements ocrés testifiant qu'il vécut.

"Que je me penche sur ta chaleur
Toi, deuxième personne ouverte,
Image à peine à moi semblable
Toi seul à savoir que je meurs."

7

Recueillons-nous pour une immémoriale nuit,
Désirs tendus, brasiers jumeaux, commun silence.
Narguons nos corps. Qu'une épée de feu nous relie!
La ville, en ses songes repue, ciel rougeoyant,

5

Uncover me as dawn uncovers a landscape,
Hold back once again the night in its shadows and let
Your blood in the morning reveal its shining.
I, I am landing—patience and passion plundered—
In the eden or hell where I was dreaming of you,
Enriching your hair with musk, and with milk
Your body, my galaxy, my moons, my sun.

Pleasure is a timeless river, its banks
Collapse to mix rock with waters.
There the heart loses its tempo and the worlds swirl
Recreating the initial chaos where our heads
Are resting in perpetual explosion, you my all . . .

6

Our story could have started in the hypothesis
Of a primordial ape with stiffened kneecaps
Gazing beyond the burnt savannas
At the last storm-cloud whitening on the horizon.
He feels a crystal vibrating in his skull, wherein flows
The measure of time, the distance, his blood,
The sands of his days and the despair
The ocher bones testifying that he lived.

"Let me lean on your warmth
You, second open person,
Image barely similar to myself
You the only one who knows I am dying."

7

Let's gather ourselves for an immemorial night,
Desires outstretched, twin fire of live coals, shared silence.
Let's taunt our bodies. Let a sword of fire connect us!
The city, in its dreams satiated, the sky reddening,

Construit ses jours futurs sur nos déjections.
Pas nous!
                    Nous voulons habiter notre maison.
Un jardin y reçoit tous les oiseaux. La porte
En est transparente.
                    Et le matin vient ranimer
Sur nos lèvres l'ardeur de nos corps à baiser.

Regards ouverts, accueillons le temps qui nous laisse
Le bonheur de nous être battus contre l'ombre
Sans verser une goutte de sang sur nos draps.

                    8
Il lacère en partant les odeurs du jardin
Comme un chat en chaleur marque son territoire.
Le citronnier flamboie d'un vert éteint, la menthe
Poivre à droite le bord du sentier jusqu'au thym.

La nuit a recélé d'insondables secrets
Le désir d'autres corps déborde tous les songes
Il regrette un fumet d'aisselles et de sang
Sa hantise depuis le tout premier matin.

          La lampe est tournée vers le mur
          Le drap relevé jusqu'au front
          Une photo montre des mains
          Un sexe lourd dans sa toison.

Is building on our dejecta its days to come.
Not us!
                    We want to live in our house.
A garden is receiving every bird. The door
Is transparent.
                    And morning comes to revive
On our lips the heat of our bodies for fucking.

With open eyes let's welcome the time that allows us
The luck of having fought against the darkness
Without spilling a drop of blood on our sheets.

                    8
Leaving he lacerates the scents of the garden
As a cat in heat marks its territory.
The lemon tree flashes a dull green light, the mint
Peppers the right edge of the path up to the thyme.

Night has hidden unfathomable secrets
The desire of other bodies overflows all the dreams
He misses a scent of armpits and of blood
His obsession since the very first morning.

            The lamp is turned toward the wall
            The sheet drawn up to the forehead
            A photograph shows hands
            A sex heavy in its mop.

Collage

* À peindre cet éloignement
Qui auréole de non-être
Au plus profond des perspectives
Ce visage aussi flou qu'il est vu
Dans le souvenir
Puis s'estompant
Et c'est le temps
De dormir.

* Les maisons des marins au temps des catastrophes
Devaient ainsi de leurs fenêtres à secrets
Cligner pour regarder le soleil sur la mer.
Maintenant, les pupilles pillées de lumières,
Les rameurs mutinés nous lancent des injures . . .

* Le rideau se lève la scène représente
Un homme qui est un homme qui . . .
Et grâce à la vertu de miroirs parallèles
Un homme qui est un homme qui apostrophe
La distance de sa droite à sa gaucherie.

* Nul ne sait qui est près ou loin
Visage maison arbre ou homme
Nul ne sait qui est qui ou quoi
Ce sont les yeux qui toujours nous trahissent.

* Hors cadre de mon temps pour cet instant doré
Aucun musée n'aura le chef-d'œuvre achevé.
Pas un Américain ne cachera dans ses caves
Un lendemain que n'aura signé aucun fou.

Collage

* To be painted: this remoteness
That haloes with non-being
In the deepest of perspectives
This face as blurred as it is seen
In memory
Then shading off
And it's time
To sleep.

* The sailors' houses in times of catastrophe
Should wink like that from their secret windows
To see the sun on the sea
Now, their pupils plundered of light,
The mutinous rowers heap insults on us . . .

* The curtain rises the scene represents
A man who is a man who . . .
And thanks to the virtue of parallel mirrors
A man who is a man who reprimands
The distance between his right and his left-handed clumsiness.

* Nobody knows who is near or far
Face house tree or man
Nobody knows who is who or what
It's always the eyes that betray us.

* Outside the frame of my time for that gilded instant
No museum will have the finished masterpiece.
No American will sequester in his cellar
A tomorrow that no fool will have signed.

* Tout se conjugue au prétérit
Et rien ne commence
Rien qui n'est pas absolument
À la minute précédant rien:
Le polygone dans ses lignes
Le cadavre entre les signes
Le brouillard dans mon désir.

* Je tiens l'épaule appuyée
Sur l'épaule appuyée. Je tiens
Les sphères de mon monde extérieur
Trop verni pour qu'y plongent mes yeux . . .
Vers quoi va le soleil
Le vénérable Verbe
Berçant cet animal la crinière enthousiaste?

* Par un subterfuge de cause à effet
Et de cause aux causes—
Suite gyroscopique ou spirale tournant
Aux notes d'une valse à façon d'alcool—
Devait naître et naquit la satiété hâtive
De boire et d'aimer et de penser normalement.
Mais argument rendu flou ou lassitude du coude
Il n'y eut de comparable à cette spontanée
Catastrophe un soir de bar
Que le processus d'auto-création
De Dieu.

* Un doigt sur les lèvres Adieu . . .
Puis cheminant à travers toits
La main sur les yeux et ta bouche
Adieu . . . jusqu'à la prochaine nuit.

Voleur brutal d'insomnie
L'escalier te hale vers le dehors

* Everything is conjugated in the past tense
And nothing starts
Nothing which is not absolutely
In the minute preceding nothing:
The polygon in its lines
The corpse between the signs
The fog in my desire.

* I keep my shoulder leaning
Against the leaning shoulder. I keep
The spheres of my outer world
Too polished for my eyes to seize it . . .
Toward what is the sun moving,
The venerable Word
Cradling the animal with the enthusiastic mane?

* By a subterfuge from cause to effect
And from cause to causes—
Gyroscopic pursuit or spiral weaving
To the strains of a waltz in the alcoholic mode—
The premature surfeit of drinking and loving
And thinking normally would be and is born.
But, whether due to clouded arguments or weariness of elbow,
There was nothing comparable to that spontaneous
Catastrophe in a bar one evening
But the process of God's
Self-Creation.

* A finger at the lips Goodbye . . .
Then wandering among roofs
Hand on my eyes and your mouth
Goodbye . . . until the next night

Brutal thief of insomnia
The stairway hauls you out

Et la nuit te recueille
Ainsi qu'un rusé pilleur d'espalier;

Les grands gendarmes étoilés
Te voient siffler des retraites à la Lune
Mais l'ombre de ma déchirure
Tombe en permanence sur le mur d'en face

Sera demain cruelle ouverte
Tellement que si tu entrais enfin
Dans le jardin des évidences
Tu en serais horrifié

Toi-même.

And night welcomes you as
An astute pillager of espaliers;

The big starry gendarmes
See you whistle retreat to the moon
But the shadow of my laceration
Falls forever on the opposite wall

Will be so cruelly open tomorrow
That if you finally entered
The garden of obvious facts
You'd be horrified

Yourself.

Poème

Comment dit-on en ce pays Demain?
Un prince sourd s'enchante au jeu des lèvres
L'argile roule aux hanches des potiers

Entrez ici il faut que la nuit tombe
Puisque sur une claie repose tel le jour
L'odeur le calme et la couleur des pommes

En ce pays comment dit-on Amour?
Ou chaque mot décuplant son pouvoir
Écrase-t-il des idées qu'il exprime?

Ouvrez la voie aux saisons à l'instant
Que le silence à la chaleur emmèle
Chairs et cheveux mains membres et rubans

En soulevant cet amas de trophées
Vous déchirerez plus d'un monument
Et avec eux le clown méconnaissable

Debout devant le miroir joues ternies
Qui par dessus l'épaule avec candeur regarde
La cendre des diamants hier évanouis.

Poem

How do you say Tomorrow in this country?
A deaf prince is charmed by the play of lips
Clay is rolling at the potters' hips

Enter here night must fall since
The odor the stillness and the color of apples
Are resting on a wicker fruit-tray like the day

In this country how do you say Love?
Or does each word multiplying its power tenfold
Crush the ideas it expresses?

Open at once the way to the seasons
Let silence entangle
Flesh and hair hands limbs and ribbons with the heat

While lifting this pile of trophies
You'll rip up more than one monument
And with them the barely recognizable clown

Standing before the mirror cheeks dulled
Who looks with candor over his shoulder
At the ashes of the diamonds that vanished yesterday.

Entr'acte

Son rêve avec le flamboyant
Le tapis rose éclaté
Lèvres paires

Il découvre le noir clavier
Les dents l'incendie éteint
Le miroir
Un tonnerre de théâtre.

Il est seul dans la salle.

Sa mère un lait lubrique
Un relent de vestale
Sur un versant
Anesthésié.

Il descend un volcan
Glaçon glissé dans sa culotte
Ardente quand paraît l'aube

Il danse une fable orientale.

Ses baisers
Il y boit palpitations
Et bave intarissable

Il souffle aussi le soir
Las trop longtemps trop lourd
De tout savoir neutre.

Il rit sous la pluie
Dans la plaine batave.

Entr'acte

His dream with the flaming
The pink rug shattered
Even-numbered lips

He discovers the black keyboard
The teeth the extinguished conflagration
The mirror
Stage thunder.

He is alone in the hall.

His mother a libidinous milk
A musty smell of a vestal
On a slope
Anesthetized.

He climbs down a volcano
Ice cube slipped into his pants
Glowing when the sun rises

He's dancing an oriental fable.

His kisses
He drinks palpitations with them
And inexhaustible slobber.

He blows at evening also
Tired too long too heavy
With knowing everything's neutral.

He's laughing in the rain
In the Batavian plain.

Nocturne américain

L'oiseau, son nom inconnu, couvre toute la nuit
De sa similitude avec un oiseau que je nomme
Dans ma mémoire ancestrale sans parvenir à évoquer
Ce parfum ancien que dispensait son chant. Cet oiseau-ci
Me semble un ami rencontré de frais avec lequel
Les paroles jamais ne remplaceront ce brillant
Des regards échangés en dépit de toute précaution.
Il m'inonde d'un musc végétal que je recueille
À chaque conjonction de branches et il paraît
Lui-même ressentir une jouissance fraternelle
À me savoir auprès de lui frémir dans son bonheur.

La nuit la rivière appelle l'homme ancien
Protégé par les dieux bénéfiques de la nuit.
Homme debout drapé dans l'immensité
Qu'il est seul à saisir, rivière, espace, nuit,
Et qu'il perçoit comme un aigle sa proie du haut
De toute son histoire d'homme à l'écoute
Des rivières, des monts, des sentiers qu'il a tracés,
De sa marque sur la terre qu'il est seul à connaître
Pas et pensées, pierres et rivières nommées,
Homme nommé, dieux créateurs à inventer
Pour prendre l'univers comme un poisson dans ses filets.

L'auto taille dans la forêt, dans la mer d'arbres traversée,
Le chemin où sont passées des tribus désorientées
Guidées par quelque Moïse vers la terre de miel et de lait
Que chante dans l'éther un cavalier aux cheveux de plumes.
Il me fait frémir comme les cordes d'une lyre,
Il me fait ouvrir les bras devant l'aurore qui s'annonce.
Au sortir de la forêt une pluie de cendres nous attend . . .
Retarde encore ce passage, et que j'entende

American Nocturne

The bird, its name unknown, covers the whole night
With its resemblance to a bird that I name
In my ancestral memory without managing to evoke
That ancient perfume its song dispenses. This bird
Seems to me a friend newly encountered with whom
Words will never replace the brightness
Of glances exchanged despite all precaution.
It floods me with a vegetal musk that I collect
At each forking of a branch and it seems
To experience a fraternal enjoyment of its own
Knowing I'm close to it trembling in its delight.

At night the river calls to the ancient man
Protected by the beneficent gods of the night.
Man standing draped in the immensity
That he alone grasps, river, space, night,
And that he perceives like an eagle its prey from the heights
Of his whole history of a man listening
To the rivers, mountains, paths he has traced,
To his mark on the earth which he alone knows
Steps and thoughts, trees and rivers named,
Man named, creator gods to be invented
To seize the universe like a fish in his nets.

The car carves out of the forest, out of the traversed sea of trees,
The road where disoriented tribes have passed
Guided by some Moses toward the land of milk and honey
That a rider with hair of feathers sings of in the ether
He makes me tremble like the strings of a lyre
He makes me open my arms before the breaking dawn.
As we leave the forest a rain of ashes greets us . . .
Delay this passage further and may I hear

Un instant de plus le bruit de la rivière la nuit,
Au delà des arbres le pas des tribus. Que je sente
L'odeur musquée des hommes libres sur la terre . . .

One moment more the sound of the river at night,
Beyond the trees the footfalls of tribes. May I smell
The musky odor of free men on earth . . .

Entre elle et moi

Elle approchait toutes les nuits
Les pieds bandés la bouche peinte
Pour doucement souffler sur mes sourcils
Et m'éveiller sans m'effrayer

Douce amère vertu
Au ventre lisse ceint
D'une cordelette magique
Qu'il ne fallait surtout pas dénouer

Et pendant l'étreinte mes mains
Mes dents mon sexe se mouraient
De ne pouvoir résoudre ce mystère
Ni même de comprendre qu'il y en avait un

Elle s'éloignait avant le matin
Le dos lacéré les flancs ensanglantés
A pas tranquille sans sourire
Et me laissait avec les gouttes

D'un onguent tombé de sa ceinture
Au bord du lit souillé où je pouvais entendre
Le jour lourd de questions se lever.

Between Her and Me

Each night she drew near
Bandaged feet painted mouth
To blow gently on my eyebrows
And wake me without frightening me

Bittersweet virtue
With smooth waist encircled
With a magic cord that above all
Must not be untied

And during the embrace my hands
My teeth my sex were dying
Of not being able to solve this mystery
Or even know if there was one

She left before morning
Her back lacerated her sides bleeding
On quiet steps without smiling
And left me with the drops

Of an ointment fallen from her sash
On the edge of the soiled bed where I could hear
The sun rising, heavy with questions.

Récitatif et air des larmes

I   *Récitatif*

Les flammes se sont glissées
Dans nos chambres à coucher
Comme serpents chassés des buissons du Sinaï.
Elles ont fait de nos corps un subtil amalgame
De molécules rendues à l'univers originel,
Et, notre esprit ayant rejoint le choeur des anges,
Avons-nous ri et pleuré devant la terre caramélisée,
Pomme trop cuite le four était trop chaud,
Étoile réduite en cendres, à un trou noir!

Pourtant c'était un paysage
Si confortable à habiter!
De puantes fumées enténébraient les soleils,
Les lignes de crête urbaine portaient des clochers
Où le vent faisait tinter des hymnes contradictoires.
Le soir ouvert laissait passer en files
Le troupeau de fourmis vers le miel des écrans . . .
Il y avait aussi derrière des monts préservés
La trace de skis montrant le chemin vers le lac
Noir où les constellations se dédoublaient
Et le bord de la mer où nous marchions casque aux oreilles
—You remember?—pour nous protéger du fracas
Répercuté entre les pics statistiques:
Cris, pleurs arrachés aux entrailles de nos terreurs.

J'habitais un palais ancien aux moucharabiehs bleus.
Les fenêtres donnaient face aux îles sur la plage.
De mon lit je voyais les garçons nus briser la vague
Et les filles sous des parasols boire à des pailles.
J'attendais une femme en un jardin. C'était le jour.

Recitative and Aria of the Tears

I *Recitative*

The flames slipped
Into our bedrooms
Like serpents chased from the bushes of Sinai
They turned our bodies into a subtle alloy
Of molecules returned to the original universe,
And, once our minds had rejoined the angelic choir,
We laughed and wept before the caramelized earth
An apple baked too long in a too-hot oven,
Star reduced to ashes, to a black hole!

Nevertheless it was such a comfortable
Landscape to live in!
Stinking fumes darkened the suns,
The urban skylines carried steeples
Where the wind made contradictory hymns ring out.
The open evening let the flocks of ants
Pass through in single file toward the honey of TV screens . . .
There were also behind the preserved mountains
The tracks of skis showing the way to the black
Lake where the constellations unfolded
And the edge of the sea where we walked wearing headsets
You remember?—to protect us from the din
Reverberating among the peaks of statistics:
Cries, sobs torn from the entrails of our terrors.

I lived in an ancient palace with blue moucharabiehs.
The windows looked out over the beach to the islands.
From my bed I saw naked boys fend the waves
And girls under parasols drinking through straws.
I was waiting for a woman in a garden. It was the day.

Un oiseau s'installait dans le feuillage.
J'appelais sans le savoir des instants de bonheur.
Puis un matin le soleil disparu ne revint pas.
Nuit incompréhensible. La main cherchant d'autres mains
Ne rencontrait dans les rues que membres disloqués
Un mur brûlant sur lequel nos ongles lacéraient
Nous ne savions plus quelle image. Seul
Un vrombissement à vomir, une boule de feu obscur
Roulait sur les pavés et le visage des hommes.

II   *Air des larmes*

Putain aux faux cils perdus
Dans le désordre de nos lits
Qui promettait des plaisirs
Des richesse et des honneurs
Tu nous disais t'appeler Vie
Et les aveugles les sourds t'avaient crue
T'avaient suivie sans y penser
Il ne nous reste qu'à pleurer
Si nous avions encore des yeux
Dans le désordre de nos lits.

Comment effacer ce désastre?
Comment revenir au berceau
Au calme des premières eaux
À la création des astres?
Et repartir pour un autre destin
Comment rêver au lendemain
À l'autre ciel à l'autre plage
À la chaleur d'un vrai soleil
Comment fuir la ville qui brûle?
Comment revenir au berceau?

A bird settled in the foliage.
Without knowing it I called these moments of happiness.
Then one morning the vanished sun didn't come back.
Incomprehensible night. A hand groping for other hands
Found only dislocated limbs in the streets
A burning wall on which our nails scratched
An image we no longer recognized. Only
A sickening hum, a ball of dark fire
Rolled along the paving-stones and on the faces of men.

II   *Aria of the Tears*

Whore with false eyelashes lost
In the disorder of our beds
Who promised pleasures
Riches and honors
You told us to call you Life
And the blind and the deaf had believed you
Had followed you without thinking
We have nothing left to do but cry
If we still had eyes
In the disorder of our beds.

How to erase this disaster?
How to return to the cradle
To the calm of the first waters
To the creation of the stars?
And leave again for another destiny
How to dream of tomorrow
Of the other sky the other beach
Of the heat of a true sun
How to flee the burning city?
How to return to the cradle?

Oh, lac / Oh, Lake

Litanies

Plaise à la pluie d'or me couvrir car j'ai froid de métal mou
Plaise à la pluie d'or me couvrir car j'ai froid de métal mou

Plaise à la pluie d'eau me couvrir car j'ai foi de métamorphose
Plaise à la pluie d'eau me couvrir car j'ai foi de métamorphose

Plaise à l'âpre idée me nourrir car j'ai soif de mes amours fausses
Plaise à l'âpre idée me nourrir car j'ai soif de mes amours fausses

Plaise à l'après-midi me suffire car j'ai trop de mes grands jours sombres
Plaise à l'après-midi me suffire car j'ai trop de mes grands jours sombres

Plaise à la près d'ici me l'ouvrir car j'ai beau frapper à sa porte
Plaise à la près d'ici me l'ouvrir car j'ai beau frapper à sa porte

Plaise à la mer calmée se grossir car j'ai trop happé les cloportes
Plaise à la mer calmée se grossir car j'ai trop happé les cloportes

Plaise à l'âme incarnée se montrer car j'ai cru en l'âme incarnée
Plaise à l'âme incarnée se montrer car j'ai cru en l'âme incarnée

Plaise à la main fermée se montrer car j'ai tiré la lame rouillée
Plaise à la main fermée se montrer car j'ai tiré la lame rouillée

Litanies

May it please the shower of gold to cover me for I am cold from soft metal
May it please the shower of gold to cover me for I am cold from soft metal

May it please the shower of water to cover me for I have faith of
    metamorphosis
May it please the shower of water to cover me for I have faith of
    metamorphosis

May it please the harsh idea to nourish me for I thirst after my false loves
May it please the harsh idea to nourish me for I thirst after my false loves

May it please the afternoon to suffice me for I've had too much of my
    dark days
May it please the afternoon to suffice me for I've had too much of my
    dark days

May it please the near here to open for me for I've knocked at its door in
    vain
May it please the near here to open for me for I've knocked at its door in
    vain

May it please the calm sea to swell for I've trapped too many sea-lice
May it please the calm sea to swell for I've trapped too many sea-lice

May it please the incarnate soul to show itself for I have believed in the
    incarnate soul
May it please the incarnate soul to show itself for I have believed in the
    incarnate soul

May it please the closed fist to show itself for I've drawn the rusty blade
May it please the closed fist to show itself for I've drawn the rusty blade

Plaise à l'amant l'aimé se mentir car j'ai su le poids du mensonge
Plaise à l'amant l'aimé se mentir car j'ai su le poids du mensonge

Plaise à l'homme enlarmé se meurtrir j'ai hurlé le cri de mes songes
Plaise à l'homme enlarmé se meurtrir j'ai hurlé le cri de mes songes

May it please the lover the loved to lie to itself for I've known the weight
of the lie

May it please the lover the loved to lie to itself for I've known the weight
of the lie

May it please the man in tears to bruise himself I've howled the cry of my
dreams

May it please the man in tears to bruise himself I've howled the cry of my
dreams

Avant, pendant, après

J'ouvre une architecture, un herbier à la main,
Abeilles apaisées posées sur mon penon,
Le jardin pailleté, les marches effeuillées
Et la licorne lasse au haut des cheminées
Pâle, lustrant son flanc, songe, à la merci
De collégiens braillards, Platon mal digéré,
Les mains ouvertes.
Ô l'œil du jardinier, les chenets, les ruchers,
Ô moi qui entre et ne sais que rire ou pleurer . . .

Auprès de la fontaine il était bon d'inventer
Un astrolabe au bastingage d'un galion
À moins que ce ne soit le poids de votre ombrelle
Sur mon genou, ombre cassée de mon désir.
Le ciel se tait. Le cèdre insiste. Il pleut
Des phrases. Non. C'était une tentative de fuite,
Et nous restions cloués au mur des vains efforts.

Rien que la simple vie. Une étoile engloutie.
Chaque visage au loin jaillissant du cambouis.
Des yeux qui regardaient qui les regarde, qui
Vacille à tenir la distance à distance,
Qui insulte à la beauté, qui bat du tambour.
Pourquoi ces perspectives d'horreur? Pourquoi
Ne pas savoir si l'heure est vraie et à quel ciel?

Les formes se pénètrent mal. Il reste un cœur
Dehors, séché de froid. Et pour faire tenir
Jésus l'éternité durant sur la croix, notre peur.
Ô combien j'inventais de saintes incertitudes
D'élégies absorbées par un tunnel, de cris?
Chansons au fond de poches crevées, artifices
Comme je vous ai pleurés, abeilles, maisons, jardin.

Before, During, After

I open an architecture, holding an herbal,
Appeased bees lighting on my pennant,
The garden spangled, the steps losing their leaves
And the tired unicorn above the chimneys
Pale, polishing its flank, dreams, at the mercy
Of yelling schoolboys, Plato badly digested,
Hands unclasped.
O the eye of the gardener, the andirons, the apiaries,
O I who enter and don't know whether to laugh or weep . . .

Near the fountain it was good to invent
An astrolabe with the railing of a galleon
Unless it was the weight of your parasol
On my knee, broken shadow of my desire.
The sky falls silent. The cedar insists. It's raining
Phrases. No. It was an attempt at escape,
And we stayed pinned to the wall of useless efforts.

Nothing but the simple life. A submerged star.
Each face in the distance spurting out of the sludge.
Eyes that looked at who looked at them, who
Staggers to keep the distance at a distance,
Who insults beauty, who beats the drum.
Why these perspectives of horror? Why
Not know if the hour is true and to what sky?

The shapes interpenetrate badly. A heart remains
Outside, dry with cold. And to keep
Jesus on the cross throughout eternity, our fear.
O how many holy uncertainties I invented,
Elegies absorbed by a tunnel, cries?
Songs at the bottom of slashed pockets, artifices.
How I wept for you, bees, houses, garden.

Gestes obscurs

Ces gestes obscurs . . . nécessairement oubliés . . .
Dès qu'accomplis. —Michel Foucault

Espace blanc peuplé de formes vides.
Je dis tu. Je vois mon image troublée
Au fond d'un verre bu.
Paillettes dorées étoiles à mourir
Ou soleil parapluie d'artifices: ma vie.

Les autres accolés à la surface des choses
Mouches ne sachant pas qu'elles sont mortes
Depuis toujours guerriers antiques et sans nom.
Aujourd'hui je titube. Une goutte de sang
S'est glissée entre le ciel et moi

Qui me fera perdre l'image des nuages
Et croire que la pluie lavera tout.
Demain ne saura plus ce qu'était hier
Avec ses ombres debout ses promesses perdues
Dans des forêts hallucinatoires.

Sillon après sillon toujours recommencé
Je parle comme un gramophone
Aux siècles enterrés. Je cherche à quelle toile
D'araignée s'est prise ma parole
Insecte trop brillant élégances empruntées.

Obscure Gestures

Those obscure gestures . . . of necessity forgotten . . .
as soon as they are made. —Michel Foucault

Blank space peopled with empty shapes.
I say: You. I see my blurred image
At the bottom of an emptied glass.
Gold paillettes stars to die for
Or sun-umbrella of stratagems. My life.

The others intertwined on the surface of things,
Flies that don't know they've always been dead,
Ancient and nameless warriors.
Today I'm staggering. A drop of blood
Slid between the sky and me

Which will make me lose the image of the clouds
And think the rain will wash everything away.
Tomorrow will no longer know what yesterday was
With its standing shadows its lost promises
In hallucinatory forests.

Groove after groove always beginning again
I speak like a gramophone
To the buried centuries. I'm trying to find which spider web
Has trapped my words—
Too brilliant insect borrowed refinements.

Élégie

Adieu près de ces champs qu'éventrent les fumées
Et que ton bras écarte
Longtemps jusqu'à la couche inéluctable des
Adieux jusqu'au prochain
Adieu

La porte d'un rocher s'est fermée. J'ai voulu
Que n'entre ici le jour que par l'arc de tes yeux
Que ne soient désignées les limites du lieu
Que par les murs charnels que nos corps érigeaient

Ouverte mieux que fut sur le temps retrouvé
La moindre jamais montre et ses pas manifestes
Ta bouche avalait l'heure et mes dents s'y brisaient
Lorsque je pénétrais en toi par des baisers

Sous la palme épanouie de mains multipliées
La rose que tu sais parterre devenue
Embaumait le silence et tuait nos secrets
Marquant notre jardin de frayeurs apaisées

Adieu   finis les chants   éventrées les années
Et que ton corps s'éloigne
Longtemps jusqu'au regret inéluctable des
Adieux jusqu'à jamais

Elegy

Adieu near those fields that smoke disembowels
    And that your arm pushes away
For a long time until the inevitable stratum of the
        Adieus until the next
            Adieu

The door in a cliff has closed. I wanted
Daylight to enter here only through the arc-lamp of your eyes
That the limits of this place be defined only
By the carnal walls our bodies erected

Opened wider on the recaptured past than the smallest
Pocket-watch and its visible trail ever were
Your mouth swallowed the hour and my teeth broke on it
When I entered you with kisses

Under the full-blown palm of multiple hands
The rose you know, on the ground now,
Perfumed the silence and killed our secrets
Marking our garden with fear that was no longer fear

Adieu   the songs are ended   the years disemboweled
        And may your body distance itself
For a long time until the ineluctable regret of
        Adieus until forever

Le Rachat

Je suis descendu dans le carré de soleil choisir parmi les noirs produits de l'autre terre celui qui secouerait mon corps engourdi du matin celui qui laverait mes membres las celui qui nourrirait ma faim de toutes choses celui qui chanterait des refrains exotiques celui qui m'apprendrait une langue dont je ne comprendrais rien

Je voulais qu'il fût solide et de bonne denture je voulais qu'il s'appelât Témérité et sût sourire qu'il dansât quelquefois dans les clairs de lune et invoquât une divinité dont l'image ornait sa chambre à la place du miroir

Or parmi le lot d'enchaînés parmi le cuivre le marbre l'ébène l'azur l'or et les parfums de ces corps mûrissant à midi je ne trouvais qu'une femme qui remplisse à peu près le canevas de mes désirs raisonnables

Je l'achetai, je signai devant le prêteur son acte de libération je l'appelai Quasi-Témérité je voulus la mettre à l'épreuve, elle me demanda de la laver de l'endormir de lui chanter une chanson sentimentale dans la langue de mon pays qu'elle ignorait

The Buying Back

I came down into the square of sunlight to choose from among the black products of the other earth the one that would shake my body numb with morning the one that would wash all my limbs the one that would nourish my hunger for all things the one that would sing exotic refrains the one that would teach me a language of which I would understand nothing

I wanted him to be strong and with good teeth I wanted him to be named Foolhardiness and to know how to smile and dance sometimes in the moonlight and invoke a deity whose picture would adorn his room instead of a mirror

So amid the chained horde the copper the marble the ebony the lapis the gold and the perfumes of those bodies ripening at noon I found only a woman who would more or less fill the outlines of my reasonable desires

I bought her I signed before the lender her deed of liberation I called her Quasi-Foolhardiness I wanted to put her to the test, she asked me to bathe her to put her to sleep to sing her a sentimental song in the language of my country which she didn't know

Carrefour

Les décombres sont à venir.
Le ciel nocturne exaltant brillait hier
Sur des insomnies coutumières.
Le jeune homme se décide à partir
À partir d'un obscur horoscope
À la recherche d'un obscur destin
Dans le silence encourageant des dieux.

Les chemins croisés les cartes perdues
Le nom noyé dans des langues étrangères
Qu'ignoraient sa mère et son père.
Le jeune homme prend son sac et son bâton
S'en remet au hasard, à sa bonne fortune,
Virevolte et loin de ses troupeaux
Marche vers sa première rencontre.

C'est une femme et c'est un chien
Elle sourit et elle jappe
Chantant parmi des ossements épars
Ce qui ressemble à l'absurde question
Que le jeune homme ne s'est jamais posée
À laquelle il répond sans réfléchir.
Le ciel tombe comme une nuit sur ses épaules
La femme-chien se meurt dans un long hurlement.

Et quand il veut s'en retourner hier s'embrouille.
Il n'y a plus d'arbre ni d'étoile ni de lit
Ni de femme ni de question ni d'horoscope.
Le carrefour n'est qu'une ligne sans hasard.
Rien ne bouge un fil se dessine rouge
Devant le soleil. Les décombres
Commencent à fumer comme jadis jamais.

The Crossroads

The rubble is still to come.
The exciting night sky was shining yesterday
On the usual fits of insomnia.
The young man decides to go away
Away from an obscure horoscope
In search of an obscure destiny
In the encouraging silence of the gods.

The intersecting routes the lost maps
The name drowned in foreign languages
His father and mother never knew.
The young man takes his sack and his stick,
Leaves it all to chance, to his good luck,
Spins around, and, far from his flocks
Walks toward his first meeting.

It's a woman and it's a dog
She smiles and she yaps
Singing amid the scattered bones
Something resembling the absurd question
The young man has never asked himself
Which he answers without thinking.
The sky falls like a night on his shoulders
The dog-woman dies inside a long howl.

And when he tries to return, yesterday is tangled.
There is no more tree or star or bed
Or woman or question or horoscope.
The crossroads is only a line without risk.
Nothing moves, a thread stands out, red
Against the sun. The rubble
Starts to smoke as in the past never.

Poème chocolat

J'étais dans un cercueil vous savez
J'essayais d'allumer ma lampe de chevet
Mais l'électricité était en grève cet été
L'ascenseur même ne descendait plus
Soyons sérieux
Le téléphone n'est pas fait pour les apôtres
Rien ne bouge d'ailleurs dans la rue
Le bruit d'un talon demeure suspendu
J'aurais pu dormir jusqu'à midi
Les éboueurs ne m'auraient pas réveillé
Ni le boucher qui dit bonjour au boulanger
Ni Justin
Je serais entré dans le magasin
Un bouquet dans la vitrine près d'une bouteille de vin
Comme je n'attends personne
Il n'y a pas de raison d'offrir des fleurs ni à boire
Soyons sérieux
Il s'agissait de chrysanthèmes que je déteste
Car ils me rappellent le Japon que je hais
Parce que tout y est baigné de pluie gris-bleu
Et que je n'y suis jamais allé
Ces bulbes chevelus cachent une absence de visage
Et pourtant j'ai beaucoup voyagé même en rêve
Au pied du vase une enveloppe non cachetée
À l'intérieur de laquelle je m'attendais à trouver
Une carte
Contenait une page arrachée à mon
Carnet de comptes
Mais au verso le papillon l'inéluctable
Mauve avec au recto des vers de Verlaine   Voici
Des vleurs, des vruits des veuilles et des vranches
Poi pi poi peur poi pui poi   peur et puis poi planche

Chocolate Poem

I was in a coffin you know
I was trying to light my bedside lamp
But the electricity was on strike that summer
Even the elevator no longer went down
But seriously
The telephone wasn't invented for the apostles
Besides nothing is moving in the street
The sound of a heel remains suspended
I could have slept till noon
The road-sweepers wouldn't have wakened me
Nor the butcher greeting the baker
Nor Justin
I would have gone into the store
A bouquet in the window next to a bottle of wine
Since I'm not expecting anyone
There's no reason to offer flowers or drinks
But seriously
It was actually chrysanthemums which I detest
Because they remind me of Japan which I hate
Because everything there is bathed in bluish-gray rain
And because I've never been there
Those hairy bulbs conceal an absence of face
And yet I've traveled a lot even in dreams
At the foot of the vase an unsealed envelope
Inside which I expected to find
A card
Contained a page torn from my
Account book
But on the verso the butterfly the inevitable
Mauve with on the recto some verses of Verlaine   Here are
Some vlowers, some vruits some vleaves and some vranches
Thethen thethen fear then thethen thethen fear and then thethen thingum

Soyons sérieux
J'essayais de trouver au fond des mes circonvolutions cérébrales
Le mot poème
Et je tombais toujours sur chocolat

But seriously
I was trying to find at the base of my cerebral convolutions
The word poem
And I always found chocolate

Soirée

Quand la musique prit fin ils se regardèrent
D'un bout à l'autre du salon à travers les glaces
Et se dirigèrent vers la porte en dansant intérieurement
Les feux d'artifice sur la plage achevaient d'endormir
Les enfants chercheurs de bagues ensevelies dans le sable
Et le monstre enchaîné au rocher près du phare
Fermait son œil incarnadin en ronronnant
C'était l'heure de prendre la fuite
La gare dans sa boîte et les signaux au bout du fil
Les noms lointains en italique sur la carte
Et quelle main ils ne savaient prête à saisir
Leur main à cette heure ce soir ou jamais.

Soirée

When the music ended they looked at each other
From one end of the salon to the other through the mirrors
And moved toward the door dancing inwardly
The fireworks on the beach finished putting the children to sleep
Who looked for rings buried in the sand
And the monster chained to the rock near the lighthouse
Closed his incarnadine eye and purred
It was the hour to take flight
To take the station in its box and the signals at the end of the wire
The distant names in italics on the map
And what hand they didn't know ready to seize
Their hand at that hour that evening or never.

Solitude brisée

Au hasard de la vie que ma vie reconnaît
Je dois voir fleurir un printemps en silence
Fête fanée papiers soleils baisers, l'espace
D'un fossé l'épaisseur des écrans obstinés
Qui séparent mon cœur de sa propre moitié.

Tiroirs ouverts je présente mes évidences
C'est toujours toi sortant du rêve où j'habitais
Ignorant les illusions les transparences
Et qu'un reflet de toi n'était pas mon reflet.

Nos mains vont s'occuper à combler l'intervalle
Que l'amour et la mort élargissent. Parfums
Blancs des grands matins nus quand nos enfances
Fatiguées d'inventer des appels sans écho
Retombaient côte à côte en colères domptées
Perpétuant le désespoir toujours déçu
De briser chaque solitude par des mots.

Broken Solitude

At the risk of the life that my life recognizes
I ought to see a spring bloom in silence
Faded fete papers suns kisses, the space
Of a ditch the thickness of the stubborn screens
That separate my heart from its own half.

Drawers are open I present my evidence
It's always you coming out of the dream where I lived
Not knowing illusions transparencies
And that a reflection of you wasn't my reflection.

Our hands will busy themselves with filling the gap
That love and death widen. White
Perfumes of the great naked mornings when our childhoods
Tired of inventing calls with no echo
Fell back side by side into mastered angers
Perpetuating the always disappointed hope
Of breaking each solitude with words.

Mairie du Quinzième

Il fallut écouter le pied des militaires
blesser les ronds que la valse à l'accordéon
laissait sur le pavé comme à une jonchée quand
a passé la procession
il fallut baiser le pied des militaires
sorti de sa godasse et lécher la cheville
et monter aussi haut que pouvait le permettre
leur drap à l'épreuve des sept millimètres cinq
il fallait secouer leur ventre comme un tapis
c'était le jour de grande illusion
quand ils s'évadent de leur profonde science
et jouent aux chercheurs de beaux successeurs
mais il valait mieux leur chercher le cœur
et mettre à la place un réveille-matin
qui pouvait sonner la diane en fantoche
mais n'apportait pas le café au lit
il fallait fouiller sous leurs fausses dents
chercher d'un doigt vif les diamants cachés
les chercher partout ne pas les trouver
même dans les plis de leur nudité.
Joie d'être un enfant du peuple souverain
de prêter la main aux institutions
et de voir son nom inscrit sur l'ardoise
des urinoirs en lettres de coaltar
pour un seul drapeau qu'on est devenu
battant son ennui au coin de deux rues
que le vent agite si ce n'est d'abord
le vent des trompettes tout amour dehors

Town Hall, Fifteenth Arrondissement

You should have heard the soldiers' feet
wounding the swirls that the accordion waltz
left on the pavement like a mower's swath
once the parade had passed
you should have kissed the soldiers' feet
pulled out of their boots and licked the ankles
and climbed as far as the khaki
seven and a half millimeters thick would allow
you should have shaken their belly like a carpet
it was grand illusion day
when they escape their deep knowledge
and pretend to look for handsome successors
but it would be better to look for the heart
and put an alarm clock in its place
that could play reveille like a puppet
but wouldn't serve coffee in bed
you should have rummaged under their false teeth
to hunt for hidden diamonds with lively fingers
hunt for them everywhere not find them
even in the creases of their nakedness.
Joy of being a child of the sovereign people
of lending a hand to institutions
and seeing one's name inscribed on the slate
of urinals in letters of coal tar
for a single flag that one has become
flapping its boredom at the angles of two streets
that the wind stirs unless it's first
the wind of trumpets all love to the winds

Bastille

Tu laissas ta chemise pencher
ses airs de manchette
au bord de la nuit qui finissait
comme une java par de doubles ritournelles
comme en la cage des matins encore clos
les canaries chantaient qu'il importait
peu que leurs fenêtres fussent ouvertes
les pierres les pavés les chambranles les charpentes
les châssis les draps du lit revêtus de leurs couleurs
battaient l'aube avec nous
meilleurs tambours que ton ventre
meilleurs bâtons que mes doigts
et les arbres et les toits la rivière et ses ponts
les lointains clairs de la ville les usines sans fumées
lavés comme à leur naissance balbutiaient
un bonjour d'essai
qui ne s'achevait pourtant
qu'en ce mot rond comme un louis
posé au bord de ce jour
par un ami délicat
le soleil sur tes bras nus contre mes joues
bonjour que je te disais
le jour du quatorz'juillet

Bastille

You let your shirt hang down
putting on airs of cuffs
at the edge of ending night
like the end of a java with double ritournelles
or the way the canaries in the cage of still-closed mornings
were singing that it mattered little
to them that their windows were open
the stones the paving stones the door-frames the armatures
the window-frames the sheets of the bed clothed in their colors
were beating the dawn along with us
better drums than your belly
better drumsticks than my fingers
and the trees and the roofs the river and its bridges
the clear distances of the city the factories without smoke
bathed as at their birth stammered
a trial hello
that only ended however
in this word round as a doubloon
placed on the edge of that day
by a considerate friend
the sun on your arms naked against my cheeks
hello I said to you
the day of quatorz'juillet

Allée-venue

Aussi longtemps que vous croyez aux miracles
Vous regardez le soleil tomber dans la mer
Chaque soir
Puis vous tournez le dos et vous enfoncez
Parmi les fougères scintillant d'une lune ou de l'autre
La nuit jusqu'aux genoux sous la voûte de cris.

Les singes pubères, les pumas adolescents
Contemplent le fin croissant
De la Terre
Dans les yeux d'une vipère crevée
Qui noue sur le macadam
L'alpha d'un futur alphabet.

C'est la fin de la nuit les moustiques
Se posent sur le front et y meurent avec vous
Dans les ruines de vos rêves érigées
Par les lointaines suggestions de villes
Où vous voulez trouver un lit
Vide pour y mourir.

Les cathédrales les cinémas les soliloques
L'oreille au violon collée d'un mendiant
Musique
Pour languir lorsque les mélodies
Vont toutes hétaïres toute ivresse pour deux sous—
Finir dans la fente rose d'un juke-box.

L'espoir est sous la main cette faible chair
Palpée massée turgescente yeux fermés
Va et vient
Que l'on garde pour soi longtemps baisers noués
Jusqu'à ce qu'un autre jour efface
La trace de chaque passage.

Coming and Going

As long as you believe in miracles
You watch the sun fall into the sea
Every evening
Then you turn your back and sink
Among the ferns sparkling from a moon or from the other
Night up to your knees under the vault of cries.

The pubescent monkeys, the adolescent pumas
Contemplate the slender crescent
Of the earth
In the eyes of a dead viper
That knots on the asphalt
The alpha of a future alphabet.

It's the end of night the mosquitoes
Place themselves on your forehead and die with you
In the ruins of your dreams erected
By the distant suggestions of cities
Where you wish to find an empty
Bed to die in.

The cathedrals the cinemas the soliloquies
The beggar's ear glued to the violin
Music
To be lovesick by when the songs
All temple prostitutes all rotgut for two cents
Are going to end up in the pink slit of a jukebox.

Hope is under the hand that weak flesh
Groped massaged turgescent with eyes shut
Comes and goes
Let's keep knotted kisses to ourselves for a long time
Until another day erases
The trace of each passing.

Sans rime ni raison

d'après un poème d'Eugene Richie

Il n'y a rien qu'un livre en langue étrangère.
Quelqu'un l'a lu et l'a refermé sur la table,
L'a oublié, s'en est allé.

Rien qu'un pont de lianes qui permet d'arriver
Dans une lumière une savane inhabitée
À mi-chemin d'un vertigineux abîme.

Rien que rires voix chinoises flottant
Le lendemain dans l'air incompréhensibles
La mémoire la musique pour toujours déchirées.

Qui que tu sois aie l'œil sur le gorille
En toi tambourinant près de ton cœur
As-tu vraiment parlé jamais à qui tu aimes?

Tout le monde est réuni dans cette gare
Dehors le vent ride sauvagement le lac.
L'après-midi s'échappera-t-elle de nouveau sans nous?

Une presque pleine lune en nuages soufrés
Monte derrière l'arbre au nom à inventer
Suffit-il de sonner l'appel pour être quitte?

Ou bien mieux vaut rester sur sa natte, à rêver . . .

Without Rhyme or Reason

after a poem by Eugene Richie

There's nothing but a book in a foreign language.
Somebody read it and shut it on the table,
Forgot it, went away.

Nothing but a bridge of vines that gets you to
A light an uninhabited savannah
Halfway to a vertiginous abyss.

Nothing but laughter Chinese voices floating
Incomprehensible in the air the next day
Memory, music torn to pieces for good.

Whoever you are keep an eye on the gorilla
In you drumming its fingers near your heart.
Have you really ever spoken to the one you love?

Everyone has come together in this station.
Outside the wind savagely ruffles the lake.
Will afternoon escape once more without us?

An almost full moon in sulfurous clouds
Rises behind the tree whose name will have to be invented.
Will the bugler playing taps settle our debt?

Or perhaps it's better to stay on one's mat, dreaming . . .

Dix Ans par exemple après

Dix ans par exemple après le jour même
Où, reflet d'une nuée parmi les branches,
Je me serais éloigné d'eux au crépuscule
Parce qu'on ne pouvait tel que j'étais devenu
Me garder sans raison apparente parce que
Justement il était désormais trop tard pour moi.

D'autres auraient pu penser qu'il est toujours trop tôt
Pour atteindre cette aube sans nous douter de rien
Pas même d'être absent dix ans dix jours dix siècles
Pour que ces branches ces nuages ce reflet
Ne puissent entrer en nous qui ne serions plus là.

Il est dur d'imaginer que ni mes yeux
Ni la moindre couleur au monde
Ni le mot œil ni le mot monde
Seraient plus
Rien sans parler des songes et du cœur unique qui bat.

Attends d'être dehors face à face avec nul ne sait quel néant
Quel inimaginable toujours jamais personne
Que tu ne seras même pas là pour goûter.

Ten Years for Example After

Ten years for example after the very day
When, a reflection of a large cloud in the branches,
I would have left the others at dusk
Because in my present state no one could have
Kept me without an apparent reason because
It was from now on precisely too late for me.

Others might have thought that it's always too soon
To reach that dawn without suspecting anything
Not even being away ten years ten days ten centuries
So that these branches these clouds this reflection
Could no longer be in us who would no longer be here.

It's hard to think that neither my eyes
Nor the smallest color in the world
Nor the word eye nor the word world
Would be nothing
Not to mention the dreams and the one heart that beats.

Wait to be outside facing who knows what nothing
What unimaginable always never anybody
That you won't even be there to taste.

Oh, lac . . .

Peur exquise envahissante dès que la nuit
Quitte les villes assoupies et que j'attends
Paré tel un oiseau soulevant le soleil
Un jour nouveau séparer les nuées.

L'heure passe et d'elle à moi se tend
La profonde chaleur de nos bouches
Et je touche ces chairs corruptibles
Elle et moi combustion promise au déchet.

Tout passé dira-t-elle allusion au poète.
La musique entre nous distillée retournera
Sans aucun doute à ce silence obscène
Que nous avons connu dans l'égoïste coït.

Alors quand séchera sur nos yeux le sang
De tant de blessures à nos cœurs infligées
Nous laisserons la nuit permanente achever
Son lent travail de destruction en nous . . .

Je l'ai placée dans un cercueil de miroirs
Magnifiant ses traits à la pâleur croissante.

Un ruban zinzolin pour le deuil de l'espoir.

Oh, Lake . . .

Exquisite invasive fear just as night
Leaves the dozing cities and I wait,
Adorned like a bird lifting the sun,
For a new day to disentangle the clouds.

The hour passes and from her to me stretches
The deep warmth of our mouths
And I touch this corruptible flesh
She and I combustion soon to be rubbish.

Everything passes she'll say (allusion to the poet).
The music distilled between us will no doubt return
To this obscene silence
We felt during selfish copulation.

Then when the blood of so many wounds
Inflicted on our hearts dries on our eyes
We'll let permanent night finish
Its slow work of destruction inside us . . .

I placed her in a mirrored coffin
To magnify the growing pallor of her features.

A reddish-purple ribbon to mourn the death of hope.

Sérénité

La grâce d'une passion sans tempête m'est échue
Et je ne l'ai demandée à personne.
Ainsi soudain se reçoivent des grâces
En une rédemption extravagante, avant le péché.

Je l'agrée comme une manne sur ma gourmandise,
Je l'absorbe par toutes les issues de mon âme.
Je me laisse habiter par ce rythme hors de ma mesure,
Et m'enlever au-delà de toute résolution.

Quelle sérénité naît de cette franchise avec moi-même!
Le tremplin du réel est donc inutile à mon essor?
Que d'amplitude à cette communion!
L'élan mystique de cette gratuite confiance!

Car j'aurais pu ne connaître de l'amour
Qu'un ciel de pleurs surplombant un lac d'orages
Et me perdre sous ces vagues et me damner
Comme ces sombres corps autour de la barque du Dante.

Le plaisir ne m'aurait peut-être pas été compté
Mais j'aurais été envahi de nausées
Après tant de tristes connivences
Lorsque j'aurais dû céder à tant de tentations.

Et je goûte aujourd'hui le pain de ma chance
Tout mon cœur s'affermit de cette nourriture
Mon corps atteint déjà la cime de ces grands arbres
Dont les feuilles vibrent de joie au vent de la vie.

Serenity

The grace of a passion without storms has been granted to me
And I asked no one for it.
Thus blessings and an extravagant reprieve
Are received sometimes, before the sin is committed.

I accept it like manna for my gluttony,
I absorb it through all the openings of my soul.
I let this rhythm beyond my limits live in me,
And carry me beyond every resolution.

What serenity flows from this frankness with myself!
So I don't need reality's trampoline for flight?
What amplitude to this communion!
The mystic surge of this granted trust!

For I could have known love only
As a sky of tears overhanging a lake of storms
And sunk under the waves and been damned
Like those dark bodies circling Dante's barque.

Maybe pleasure wouldn't have been charged to my account
But nausea would have entered me
After so much sad conniving
When I'd have given in to so many temptations.

And today I taste the bread of my good luck
This food makes my heart grow stronger
Already my body has reached the tops of those tall trees
Whose leaves vibrate with joy in the wind of life.

Vin

Les fleurs que j'ai plantées le long de ma route
Ont duré longtemps malgré vents et froidures
Déjà midis ardents commencent à brûler
Sournoisement le secret des racines
Et je sais qu'il ne restera de mes pas
Qu'une trace une grappe une goutte
Pour rappeler par les sentiers que j'ai choisis
Ces soirs où la lumière chantait
Dans les yeux les mains les cœurs et les verres.

J'aime sur la langue l'âpreté douce
Emplissant le palais d'une salive promise
Butant sur le clavier muet des dents
Avec des draperies levées dont on dirait
Que la mémoire en gardera une traînée fugitive
Entre-aperçue on ne saura comment ou bien
L'éclatant rappel du moment unique
Toute pesanteur abolie retrouvé l'inconscient
Plaisir de n'être que pleinement animal.

Car notre vie fermée sur cette sphère chatoyante
Couleur goût et parfum à leur extrême invoque
Quelque miracle indépendant de la genèse
Produite par distillation de l'air et de la terre—
Telle la démarche vers des planètes technologiques
Venue d'un calcul fait sur les doigts d'une main—
Temps contenu coulant—continuel automne
Ce soir ce vin qui entre en moi pour me faire
La tête légère le verbe prolixe le sexe heureux.

Wine

The flowers I planted along my road
Have lasted long despite winds and cold
Already fiery noons begin to burn
Slyly the secret of the roots
And I know that of my footsteps nothing will remain
But a trace a cluster a drop
To recall along the paths I've chosen
Those evenings when the light sang
In eyes hands hearts and goblets.

I love the sweet harshness on the tongue
Filling the palate with a promised saliva
Knocking the mute keyboard of the teeth
With raised draperies of which one might say
That memory retains a fleeting trail of them
Half-glimpsed we won't know how or else
The loud reminder of the single moment
All gravity banished the unconscious pleasure recaptured
Of being nothing but entirely animal.

For our life closed on that iridescent sphere
—Color taste perfume at their extreme limits—invokes
Some miracle independent of its origin
Produced by distilling air and earth—
Like the move toward technological planets
After a calculation made on the fingers of one hand—
Time contained flowing—continual autumn
This evening this wine that enters me to make
My head light my tongue loose my cock happy.

D'un domaine privé

J'irai compter mes troupeaux dispersés
Vivante allusion à mes pères innombrables
Mais comment atteindre au nombre d'étoiles
Peintes jusqu'aux bornes éloignées de la pensée?

Des fleuves au-delà coulent fuite ou couronne
Phantasmes enrichis de toucher de parfum
Ils laissent espérer un goût de baiser mûr
Un regret une pomme tombée ou la pluie.

Pourquoi humer ici la pourriture exquise
Soulever les jupons ancestraux découvrir
Peut-être regretter des questions oubliées?

Le domaine est bien clos aussi loin que l'on veuille
Pour se sentir moins seuls par les nuits qui nous restent
Pour voir plus loin pour deviner une autre compagnie.

From a Private Domain

I'll go count my scattered flocks
Living allusion to my innumerable fathers
But how do I attain to the number of stars
Painted as far as the distant boundaries of space?

Out there, rivers flow—flight or crown—
Phantasms gifted with the sense of touch with perfume
They let you hope for a taste of ripe kisses
A regret a fallen apple or the rain.

Why inhale the delicious rot here
Lift ancestral petticoats to discover,
Perhaps to regret, forgotten questions?

The domain is fenced in as far as we wish,
To feel less alone in the nights remaining to us,
To see farther to recognize other companions.

Une Visite

Dans sa hâte d'approcher l'Arbre
—Ses bandes déroulées, ses aromates,
Par la forêt blanche un ronron d'après-midi—
La personne
Hermine au corps blanc piqueté d'entailles
Où le givre s'amenuise,
S'est brisé le crâne à coups de poing.
Araignée vide de fil, pendule encore horrifié,
Mesure d'univers compact, de toute nuit . . .

C'était la première fois que je ne dormais pas seul.
J'appelais son nom, mâchoires disloquées.
Des enfants sous le parapluie parlaient d'oranges
Dansaient autour de fontaines solidifiées
Devant des fenêtres pour longtemps fermées.
Elle toucha mon ventre
Et sa main bleuit.
Une page entière en devint illisible
Où se mêlaient cartes postales constellées
Rivages vus du bastingage, et savanes.
Alors je commençais à voir que je perdrais
Si je ne parlais tout de suite
Je m'obligeais à demeurer en moi.

Ah! peindre les jours banals, noces, visite à l'accouchée!
Semer sous les portes les branches folles du téléphone
Fixer, dater, numéroter la place où je suis
Chambres, zoos, dancings, dômes éclatés, bagarres . . .
Je sors, je pelote en taxi d'ex-divas et je prends forme
Au creux de leur coude levé à table autour d'une musique.
Irremplaçable pourriture, machine gaspillée,
Sommeil absent, train dégueulasse,
Façade frottée contre le vent.

A Visit

In her haste to approach the Tree
—Its peeling bark, its spices,
Through the white forest a hum of afternoon—
The person
Ermine whose white body pricked with black cuts
Where the frost dwindles,
Has cracked its skull with blows of the fist.
Spider emptied of thread, still-horrified clock,
Measure of a compact universe, of the whole of night . . .

It was the first time I hadn't slept alone.
I cried out her name, my jaws dislocated.
Children under the umbrella spoke of oranges
Danced around solidified fountains
In front of windows that had long been shut.
She touched my belly
And her hand turned blue.
A whole page of it turned unreadable
On which were mingled constellated postcards
Landscapes seen from the ship's rail, and savannahs.
Then I began to see that I would lose
Unless I spoke immediately.
I forced myself to stay within myself.

Ah! to paint the ordinary days, weddings, visits to the maternity ward!
To plant under doors the wild branches of the telephone
To fix, date, number the place where I am
Bedrooms, zoos, dance halls, broken domes, brawls . . .
I go out, I grope ex-divas in taxis and take shape
In the hollow of their elbow raised at table around some music.
Irreplaceable rot, wasted machine,
Absent sleep, disgusting train,
Facade rubbed against the wind.

Tu t'assieds. Serpent. Au cou l'ombre
De fourches trace une issue.
Fleur rouge et bleue le laid volubilis
Comme toi siffle. L'oiseau lointain
Jette sa première pierre ou joue de la harpe.
J'étais venu pour voir s'évanouir
Ma jumelle hardie tirée du songe
Et je me trouve porté sur l'œil
À prendre un verre qui s'irise franchissant les ères
La tête enveloppée des bandelettes d'aromates
Quand les enfants parlent d'oranges
Autour de bavardes fontaines.

You sit down. Serpent. At your neck the shadow
Of forks traces an exit.
Red and blue flower the ugly convolvulus
Like you, whistles. The distant bird
Throws its first stone or plays the harp.
I had come to watch the swoon
Of my bold twin pulled from the dream
And I find I am drawn to the eye
To have a drink that grows iridescent as it crosses the ages
My head wrapped with strips of spices
When the children speak of oranges
Around the garrulous fountains.

Ballade

Mes écuyers cavalcadours
Mes cent visages sous un heaume
Un seul percheron chevauchez
Mes écuyers cavalcadours
Un seul visage présentez
Sous cent heaumes d'argent niellé.

À l'heure des spectres glissant
En fleuve visqueux hors des tombes
Mes écuyers cavalcadours
Escortez la litière basse
À l'heure où toutes raisons glissent
Vers l'ouvert jardin de mes rêves.

Anges gardiens aux pas ouatés
Custodes aux armes tranchantes
Mes écuyers cavalcadours
Heaumes baissés sur vos regards
Veillez sur mon sommeil troublé
Je veillerai sur votre heaume.

Veillez mais veillez donc! Veillez
Mes écuyers cavalcadours
Aux vendeurs de plaisirs faciles
Aux voleurs de baisers ardents
Aux conteurs de fausses histoires
Embusqués sur notre itinéraire.

Et que j'arrive à mon jardin
Près de fontaines où voir enfin
Mes escorteurs aux cent visières
Votre incognito soulevé

Ballad

My cavaliers my equerries
My hundred faces under a helmet
Straddle a single percheron
My cavaliers my equerries
Reveal a single face
Under a hundred silver-inlaid helmets.

At the hour of specters sliding
In a viscous river out of tombs
My cavaliers my equerries
Escort the low-slung litter
At the hour when all reasons slide
Toward the open garden of my dreams.

Guardian angels with padded feet
Custodians with slicing arms
My cavaliers my equerries
Helmets lowered over your gaze
Watch over my troubled sleep
I'll watch over your helmet.

Watch but keep on watching! Watch out
My cavaliers my equerries
For sellers of easy pleasures
For stealers of burning kisses
For tellers of false tales
In ambush along our route.

And see that I reach my garden
Near the fountains where at last I can see
My escort with a hundred visors
Your incognito lifted

Refleté dans mes propres yeux
Mon seul visage qui me gardait.

Mes écuyers cavalcadours
Mes écuyers cavalcadours
Mes écuyers cavalcadours . . .

Reflected in my own eyes
My only face which protected me.

My cavaliers my equerries
My cavaliers my equerries
My cavaliers my equerries . . .

Uncollected Poems

Eau calme

Des larges galions d'argent jettent l'ancre sans rider
La surface des eaux du havre de toutes grâces
Et la deuxième nef s'immobilise, voiles dormant.

Ce n'est pas un reflet mais une tangible
Et vraie carène illuminée de glauque,
Tenue sous l'autre comme bouche à bouche,
Plus que soeur, la même carène.

Sans solliciter de forme précise, par le miracle
Des abandons à la pureté des bilatéralismes
Se réalise l'harmonieuse unité.

Et hors la matière iodée des solives, demeure,
Après soleils couchés, vagues au loin
Cette éternelle dualité sans trait d'union,
Cette bouche dans cette bouche.

Calm Water

Wide galleons of silver weigh anchor without wrinkling
The water's surface in the harbor of all grace
And the second ship comes to a stop, sails asleep.

It's not a reflection but a true
And tangible keel, illuminated, sea-green,
Held under the other one as mouth to mouth,
More than a sister, the same keel.

Without seeking a precise shape, through the miracle
Of surrenders to the purity of bilateralisms,
The harmonious singleness comes into being.

And beyond the iodized material of the joists, it stays,
After set suns, vague in the distance,
This eternal duality with no hyphen,
This mouth in this mouth.

Connivences

Minute noire et verte, en onde, aboutissant
À deux mains de cellophane, penchées,
Comme des fleurs sans eau.

Espace de mes yeux, tu imposes des écluses
De silence aux flots paralléles d'évasion:
La certitude d'une sympathie m'est acquise.

Et quand j'écarte comme un rideau
Mes doigts de chair, quelqu'un peut rire:
Il a perdu. Je me suis inventé un ami
                    Sans visage.

Collusion

Black and green minute, in waves, ending
In two cellophane hands leaning
Like flowers without water;

Space of my eyes, you impose sluice-gates
Of silence on the parallel waves of escape;
I've gained the assurance of a sympathy.

And when I part, like a curtain,
My fingers of flesh, someone can laugh. He has lost:
I've invented for myself a friend
               Without a face.

Petit matin

Est-ce toi? C'est la nuit. L'escalier a plié. Les portes sont soudées aux chambranles. Les horloges tuées. La ciel de minuit n'avait de lune qui vaille. Est-ce toi? C'est pour moi. Ce n'est toi. À demain.

Puis je te recontrai sur le trottoir et des fourmis en ta cervelle. "Ils ne m'ont pas voulue mais ils m'ont tout volé. S'ils m'avaient voulue je leur aurais tout donné."

Puis tu te revêtis de ta dernière robe. "Je ne sais. Je ne veux. Non pas par les boulevards" et comme je dormais entre midi et l'aube tu montas jusqu'au toit en passant par chez moi. Tu montas par le mur comme un autre lézard.

Tu glisses au soleil sans sandale et sans peigne. Donnez ce qu'ils ont pris. Est-ce toi cet amas. Un linge de coton cache le trou du jour.

Early Morning

Is it you? It's night. The stairway has folded. The doors are soldered to their frames. The clocks killed. The midnight sky had no moon worth bothering with. Is it you? It's for me. It's not you. Till tomorrow, then.

Then I met you on the sidewalk and ants in your brain. "They didn't want me but they stole all I had. If they had wanted me I'd have given them everything."

Then you put on your last dress. "I don't know. I don't want to, not by the boulevards" and as I was sleeping between noon and dawn you climbed up to the roof passing my room. You climbed the wall like another lizard.

You slip into the sunlight without a sandal or a comb. Given what they took from you. Is it you that pile. A cotton cloth covers the day's hole.

Histoire non naturelle

Une anachronique chimère fardée de strass maigre à souhait vendait son lustre—pendeloques—devant la façade allumée d'un magasin de porcelaine et les marchands de journaux frais la bousculaient sans qu'elle parut se soucier des bruits de la rue du mouvement lent des maisons ou de la rotation du ciel.

Le ruisseau portait un bateau fait d'un fétu voile de soie. Le papier à lire l'amour coulait sur les vagues vers les égouts ouverts comme un jour de semaine entre l'heure du loup et l'heure du berger. Les passants posaient le pied sur les clous du soir. Chaque signal d'aller de l'avant était fixé à leur revers.

Puis le défilé des sorcières passa le moins inaperçu. Sur le char d'un choeur angélique la guimauve des voix catthareuses. Leur sourcil peint leur dent étiquetée leurs doigts alourdis d'ongles verts. Quand elles criaient Evohe l'écho des murs disait Cent francs l'écho des montagnes Jamais l'écho de l'horizon Achtung.

Et le silence drapa les statues du rouge des pudeurs sincères. Loin du foin sec des allumettes du corps ardent ces incendiaires. La nuit dormait à l'envie des enseignes lumineuses. La palme du martyre fut décernée à la patiente car elle avait vomi tous les secrets de son tronc sur la chaussée.

Vidée comme un sac retournée comme une seiche et l'os que l'on voyait maintenant blanc coulait en rivière nappait de crème le gâteau de ses viscères. Elle se décida lentement lentement à mourir et demanda entrant au portier du ciel la grâce que sa pierre soit gravée d'une série de chiffres romains et serve de cadran solaire.

Unnatural History

An anachronistic chimera camouflaged with rhinestones, as scrawny as one could wish, was hawking her chandelier (crystal pendants) before the lighted façade of a porcelain shop and the vendors of fresh newspapers jostled her without her seeming to mind the noise of the street the slow motion of the houses or the rotation of the sky.

The stream carried a boat made from a straw with a sail made of silk. The paper to read love on flowed on the waves toward the sewers open as on weekdays between the hour of the wolf and the hour of the shepherd. Pedestrians placed their feet on the studded crosswalks of evening. Each signal to go forward was pinned to their lapels.

Then the parade of witches passed, barely noticed. On the float of an angelic choir, marshmallow sweetness of catarrhal voices. Their painted eyebrows their labeled teeth their fingers weighed down with green fingernails. When they cried Evoé the echo from the walls came back, "One hundred francs." Never an echo from the horizon Achtung.

And the silence draped the statues with the red of sincere modesty. Far from the desiccated hay the matches the ardent bodies—these arsonists. Night slept, vying with the neon signs. The martyr's crown was bestowed on the patient since she had vomited all the contents of her poor-box onto the pavement.

Emptied like a sack flipped over like a cuttlefish the bone one now saw was white flowed in a river napping with cream the cake of her viscera. She slowly decided to die and entering heaven's gate asked the porter as a favor to have her stone engraved with a series of Roman numerals and that it be used as a sundial.

Musique

Vous me tambourinez sur le crâne je ne sais quelle percussion de forêts et de détresses

Ô mains qui ouvrez le ban des circonstances à retenir

Et ce n'est pas un peuple et ce n'est pas le seul épanchement d'un solitaire sur sa tour

qui harangue, du haut des oreilles tendues, la tristesse de mes matins la longueur des jours qui me sont dûs

Et ce n'est pas un appel venu de quelque endroit qu'un jour je puisse atteindre

à grand effort d'attention comme une récompense à ma fonction d'être

qui fait vibrer les feuilles d'or qui indique à quel détour de la mémoire se cache ou se révèle un signe majestueux

bruit des autres hautes colonnes de silence amoncelées   ruines éparses du silence

entre les pierres du plafond sous les allégories indéchiffrables se joue le psaume ancien qu'il n'est pas besoin de connaître pour aimer ni d'aimer pour connaître

J'entends marcher un pas de femme sur les feuilles de l'été écoulé

J'entends soupirer un étonnement devant les clairières ouvertes comme une avenue dans un quartier pauvre

Music

You are drumming I don't know what percussion of forests and grief
into my skull

O hands beginning the ceremony of circumstances to be born in
mind

And it's not a people not the lone outpouring of a hermit on his
tower

who harangues, from the height of expectant ears, the sadness of my
mornings and the overlong days that are my due

And it's not an appeal coming from some place I'll be able to reach
some day

with a huge effort of attention like a reward for my function of
being

that makes the gold leaves vibrate that indicates at which crossroads in
my memory a majestic sign is hiding or revealing itself

noise from the pile of other tall columns of silence   sparse ruins of
silence

between the stones of the ceiling under the undecipherable allegories
the ancient psalm is being played that doesn't need to be remembered
in order to be loved nor loved in order to be remembered

I hear a woman walking on the leaves of summer that has passed

I hear amazement sighing before the deforested clearings, open like
an avenue in a poor neighborhood

J'entends tourner sur ses gonds la porte d'un temple

Et le portique s'emplit de vibrantes agitations de présence accumulée comme une vasque sous le fil d'eau de la fontaine

vent qui me rentre par l'oreille et m'accole à un arbre ainsi qu'un linge mouillé

vent qui me fait épouser les pierres

puis un chant déchiré attend la gorge qui lui donnera vie

les visages entourent les instruments de mesure, une meute désire tenir sous ses dents le calme gibier

visage et vent forment le faisceau d'inutiles complicités pour laisser ignorer les allées et venues du néant

    silence impérieux   bouchon de liège du silence sur la mer balance dessinant les hauts et les bas de vagues profondes

    roule roule   ondes écrasées   supplice de milliers d'espérances condamnées à n'être jamais qu'espérances et pourtant réunies comme une troupe de communiants

    tenez-moi longuement lieu d'appareil à vivre   instruments débordants de possibles miracles

    J'écoute un seul être posé devant les dents d'un piano qui sait ranimer les flammes les plus anciennes et appelle au rendez-vous de notre joie les morts déjà tournés en poussière qu'on respire

    Je hais l'ordonnance du monde clandestin je veux deviner le sens de tous les signes

I hear the door of a temple turning on its hinges

And the portico fills with the vibrant turbulence of accumulated presence like a basin under the thread of water from a fountain

wind that enters my ear and flattens me against a tree like a wet cloth

wind that fits my body to the stones

then a torn song waiting for the throat that will give it life

faces surround the measuring tools, a pack of hounds longs to hold the calm prey in their teeth

face and wind form the sheaf of pointless collusions that let the comings and goings of emptiness proceed unnoticed

> urgent silence   cork of silence bobbing on the sea   scales to weigh the peaks and hollows of deep waves
>
> revolve revolve   smashed waves   torture of thousands of hopes condemned to be never anything but hopes yet gathered together like a group of communicants
>
> be my lasting substitute for a machine for living   instruments overflowing with possible miracles
>
> I'm listening to a single being placed before the teeth of a piano that can revive the oldest flames and calls to the conclave of our joy the dead who've already turned to the dust we breathe
>
> I hate the order of the clandestine world I want to intuit the meaning of all signs

Je veux laisser dehors à toutes neiges les enfants mal venus d'un solitaire émoi

Nuit qui fait une tour de leurre où les canonnades se répercutent nuit passée au filtre des heures avec des promenades immobiles des plongées dans hier des essors au-dessus de demain

J'écoute un seul être posé devant ces images volées à l'album d'une famille éteinte qui dresse le décor d'une si vieille coutume

L'amant avec l'objet de son amour
La mère présente au trépas de son dernier fils

Pathétique déroulement de spires dont le bout se perd dans une embrouille de déboires

Et je m'allège de ce qui me fait contemporain de moi-même le sac de ma chair, le vêtement de sensibilité

Et je m'allonge sur le nuage prêt à crever en une pluie qui fécondera les illusoires champs d'éternité

Et je m'arrange un lit de feuilles fanées   une ambiance parfumée aux moins denses effluves   un soir sempiternel avec ce frère qui me vient chaque fois que s'ébranle pour moi un train d'ondes particulières

I want to leave outside in every snow the unwanted children
of a solitary outburst of feeling

Night that creates a decoy tower where cannon shots
reverberate   night filtered through the hours with immobile
strolls dives into yesterday flights above tomorrow

I'm listening to a single being placed before these pictures
stolen from the album of an extinct family that is building the
scenery of so ancient a custom

The lover with the object of his love
The mother present at the dying of her youngest son

Pathetic unwinding of whorls whose end is lost in a tangle of
misfortunes

And I grow lighter from what makes me a contemporary of
myself   the sac of my flesh, the garment of feeling

And I lie down on the cloud about to burst into rain that will
irrigate the illusory fields of eternity

And I make my bed of fallen leaves   an ambience scented
with the least dense effluvia   a never-ending evening with
this brother who comes to me each time a train of particular
waves is set in motion

Carrière

Pendant que l'enfant jouait au cerceau
Les dames chantaient en robe de mariée
Comptez vos boutons tirez votre sort
Un pantalon rouge attire les filles
J'embrassai ma mère et la carrière
Au bout de la route au son du canon
Ne fais pas le con Fanfan la Tulipe
On revient souvent des Flandres manchot
De Naples échaudé de Venise borgne
De Rome curé de Cologne chauve
De Yorktown cocu d'Alger maquereau
Et si l'on revient de Trocadéro
La dame rassie son derrière au vent
Demande cent sous pour en faire autant
Que gratis à qui est resté au chaud
Pendant que Fanfan crevait au héros

Career

While the child played with a hoop
The ladies were singing in their bridal gowns
Count your buttons draw your lot
Red trousers attract the girls
I embraced my mother and the new career
At the end of the road to the noise of the cannon
Don't be an jerk Fanfan la Tulipe
Often one returns one-armed from Flanders
Syphilitic from Naples one-eyed from Venice
From Rome a vicar from Cologne bald
From Yorktown a cuckold from Algiers a pimp
And if one returns from Trocadero
The sedate lady with her ass in the wind
Asks a hundred sous to do the same
Free of charge for him who stayed nice and warm
While Fanfan spilled his guts like a hero

L'Essentiel d'un visage se lit un jour de gel

L'essentiel d'un visage se lit un jour de gel
L'attirail d'inspiration les mains les clés les arbres
Le trousseau des procédés amassé temps après temps
Et brodé d'initiales flamboyantes
De papillons sans discrétion
Maintenant que dans ces limites de froidure
Se dort ta tête jeune-vieux poète
Maintenant que dans les limites de leur chair à zéro
Se tiennent empesées tes lèvres et tes joues
Maintenant que tu meus ta langue
Dans un palais de miroir
L'essentiel de ton visage se lit comme un journal.

The Main Thing in a Face Can Be Read on a Freezing Day

The main thing in a face can be read on a freezing day
The apparatus of inspiration the hands the keys the trees
The bunch of behaviors stored up time after time
And embroidered with blazing initials
With butterflies without discretion
Now that within these limits of cold
Your head is sleeping young-old poet
Now that within the limits of their flesh at zero
Your lips and your cheeks remain starched
Now that you move your tongue
In a palace of mirrors
The main thing in your face can be read like a newspaper.

Ciel scintillant

Comme si le ciel scintillant devenait
Molécule gelée ballottée dans l'espace
Un seul être éternel lui-même molécule
Un seul incommensurable esprit dernier.

À ma porte il frappa. C'était encore un soir
Suivant une journée de soleil obstiné
Qui commençait comme un prélude au rêve.
«Souris dit-il, la fin est c'est tout.»

Je regarde mes mains comme tournées en cendre
Les rouges ruisselets descendant de mon coeur
Et bleus remontant vers la machine molle
Torchon brûlant le temps à lui compté.

Scintillating Sky

As though the scintillating sky became
A frozen molecule tossed about in space,
A single eternal being, itself molecule,
A single immeasurable last spirit.

At my door he knocked. It was another evening
Following a day of stubborn sun
That began as a prelude to the dream.
Smile he said the end is the end that's all.

I look at my hands seemingly turned to ashes
The red rivulets descending from my heart
And mounting blue to the soft machine
(Trouble at home): the allotted time.

Les Soirées de Rochefort

DEPUIS QUE CES MAISONS PAR LA LOI SONT FERMÉES
((Un ancien marsouin pouvait s'y croire en Chine
(sous d'orange lueurs, lanternes oubliées
—à vingt ans, loin de Rochefort, le coeur se brise . . .
. . . il suffit d'un tafia, d'un disque, d'un baiser:
l'enseigne aisé sous le paravent s'acoquine,
mais la manche d'or vierge et le bonnet à rose
rouge, au faux jour des boules-diamants expose
la main sous l'obi, l'oeil à ce fil de mois fixé
qui, par canal, escale et passage de Ligne,
relie la porte ronde à la place Colbert
loin du regard tiré des savantes poupées).
Si les femmes ici sous un masque se cachent
—qu'il est plat leur baiser de rouge dégoûtant;
la caresse et la joue glissent sous les onguents;
leur art vénal se compare à fleur croupissante
lorsque, nues, se prêtant à profitable émoi,
elles rient du gars naïf, l'ardeur désordonnée—
elles savaient là-bas, la grège soie quittée,
(les heures se payaient en fièvres, en soleils)
fragiles sous le doigt, ivoires, noirs rubans
jouer de l'instrument, à la besogne expertes,
faire virer le cotre et tanguer la frégate,
basculer l'azimuth, limer le cacatois,
accompagnant la lente ascension à la hune,
d'un humide concert, viole, flûte et hautbois))
LES GARÇONS DE CE PORT ne connaissent la mer
(((d'anciennes nefs parmi les roseaux vifs s'envasent
qui, naguère, apportaient au calfat, au marteau,
leur coque à décaper de nacre et de coraux
. . . désormais, au Musée, un modèle prolonge
—avec ses cabestans, ses pavois, ses haubans,

Evenings in Rochefort

NOW THAT THOSE HOUSES HAVE BEEN CLOSED BY LAW
((A former marine could think himself in China
(in the orange light that falls from unwatched lanterns
—at twenty, far from Rochefort, the heart breaks . . .
. . . a glass of rum, a record, a kiss suffice:
the well-heeled ensign's debauched behind a screen
but the sleeve bare of stripes and cap with red
pompom, in false neon day, exhibits
the hand under the obi, eye on the string
of months that via canal, port, Equator
connects the round door with the Place Colbert
far from the slanted look of knowing dolls).
If here the women hid behind a mask
—how insipid is their kiss of nasty red;
the caress and cheek are slippery under salves;
their venal art is like some stagnant flower
when, nude, a prey to lucrative emotion,
they mock some naive lad's disordered ardor—
back there they knew how, once the raw silk doffed,
(the hours were paid back with fevers and with suns)
ivory, black ribbons, fragile beneath the fingers,
to play the instrument, expert at the task,
to make the cutter swerve, the frigate pitch,
to tilt the azimuth, file the mizzenmast,
accompanying their slow climb to the crow's net
with a damp concert, viol, flute, and oboe))
THE BOYS OF THIS PORT only knew the sea
(((derelicts sink in mud amid living reeds
that erstwhile brought to caulker and to hammer
their hulls to scrape off mother-of-pearl and coral
. . . henceforth, in the Museum, a model prolongs
—with its winches, rigging, decorative flags

(comme un hiéroglyphe avant Champollion
symbole mal lavé de ce qu'il représente)—
le souvenir d'odeurs, de bruits à l'Arsenal,
le cri des ouvriers découvrant dans la cale
une fleur oubliée par quelque vahiné
((telle, parée de paille eût pu voir *Mon Frère Yves*
—l'essentiel offusqué par d'ébènes cheveux,—
une reine insulaire, à vrai dire virile
(le fût bien, si l'on en croit d'autres, Azyadé))
pour qu'avec ses pavés, ses angles durs, la ville
au grand large liée par de trop longs chemins
(soeur de celle où Marie, nouvelle Bérénice,
dit adieu à Louis qui pleure pourtant roi;
de l'autre d'où partit la dernière croisade,
que lentement le temps des vagues écarta)
ressuscite, déjà morte, déjà perdue . . .)))
qu'à jeux de grâce autour d'un filet à loisir,
patience pour un peu de bronze sur la peau,
beau corps d'ici, d'ailleurs ignorant les rudesses,
Narcisses admirant leur image en autrui,
plomb pesant douleur dans leurs plus basses parures
qu'ils arborent, si peu que midi les harcèle,
sous le triangle étroit d'une infime pudeur;
qu'au roulement de vert sur ocre au cinéma
(manque pourtant le sel sur lèvre, sur coupure,
ensemble, et l'horizon qui ferme son compas,
la myriade au ciel d'étoiles familières,
même le continuel éveil d'oreille interne,
balance de la hanche et du pied assurée,
ou le sommeil, le creux de l'errante coquille
situe le coeur au coeur des routes traversées)
NE CONNAISSANT L'AMOUR QU'EN SONGE QUOTIDIEN:
fragments, toujours coupés de la plus chaude scène,
qu'accroupi l'on déchiffre aux cloisons à virgule
—Amérique ignorée, planète bien vivable—

(like a hieroglyphic before Champollion
ill-washed symbol of what it represents)—
the memory of sounds and smells in the Arsenal,
the cry of workmen finding in the hold
a flower forgotten by a Tahitian girl
((as, decked with straw, *Mon Frère Yves* might have seen her
—her essential tresses obfuscated—
an island queen, and masculine in truth
(as was, according to some, Azayadé))
so that the town, its cobbles and sharp angles
linked to the open sea by routes too long
(sister of the one where Marie, new Bérénice,
took leave of Louis, weeping though a king;
and of that from which the last crusade departed,
since then from the waves by time slowly subtracted)
may revive, already dead, already lost . . .)))
though games of quoits around a net for play,
patience for a little bronze upon the skin,
svelte local forms, of foreign asperities
ignorant, Narcissi admiring their reflections
in others, leaden pain in those low trimmings
they brandish as soon as noon harasses them,
under scant decency's slim triangle;
from green turning to ocher in the movies
(lacking, however, are salt on lip, on cut
alike, the horizon which shuts up its compass,
in the sky the myriad of familiar stars,
even the inner ear's constant attention,
equilibrium of hip and foot both thus assured,
or sleep, hollow of the erring cockleshell,
locates the heart at the heart of traveled routes)
KNOWING LOVE ONLY AS A DAILY DREAM:
fragments, the hottest scene deleted always,
that, crouching, you decipher from the comma'ed partition
—American hygiene unknown, O livable planet—

rassemblant dans le noir, au scandale voués,
empereurs impuissants, princes mal mariés,
vieux amants brûlants l'un sur l'autre un passé triste,
ventres ouverts qu'un prêtre délirant baptise ...
et pour, seul habiter ce palais de papier
le visage moqueur qu'Elle laisse admirer
((mais sous la jupe alerte et le corsage amène,
des rondeurs réservées au bonheur conjugal
avec toit, lit de ronce de noyer, armoire
à miroir, machine où mousse la sueur,
liste de matchs gagnés quand la soupière fume,
monde blême à portée des regards fatigués,
et le même chemin du soir jusqu'au matin,
la surprise émoussée sous le drap du trousseau,
refuge louchissant: l'ivresse régulière
qui multiplie la morne humeur, engorge le foie,
qui dresse le remords, papillottes aux tempes,
qui vide l'escarcelle et engendre les monstres
(l'oeil bavant, l'os de gomme, un crâne mal scellé,
un coeur percé qu'on fait guérir outre-Atlantique,
après honte et honneur de collectes publiques)
trop de petits cercueils dans des trous pourrissant,
qu'il faut aller fleurir chaque Premier novembre))
quand on peut contempler, de cire sous la vitre
quand on peut croiser dans la crique des parfums,
quand on touche le pli qu'elles ont à l'aisselle,
quand on chante plaisir à gueule de manège,
quand on lèche le rose et le bistre à leur cou
(dans les grains, pour cent francs, de l'héliogravure)
quand on erre parmi les algues emmêlées,
tournant, boussole folle au calme mal gardé,
l'ancre noire—et l'on coupe la chaîne, et l'on hurle
en vain, tant de vaisseaux gonflés de sang, soudain;
SE GROUPENT CHAQUE SOIR là où l'ancien marais
(jusqu'aux murs dont une seule échauguette appelle

re-assembling in the dark, to scandal vowed,
impotent potentates, princes poorly mated,
old lovers burning a sad past on each other,
ripped wombs baptized by a delirious priest . . .
and, so as to live alone in this paper palace
the insolent face She allows you to admire
((but alert beneath the skirt and pleasing bodice
are curves reserved for conjugal delight
with roof, burl walnut bed and tall armoire
with mirror; machine where perspiration foams;
the football scores when steams the soup tureen;
a wan world within range of weary gazes;
and the same beaten track from dusk till dawn;
the blunted surprise beneath the trousseau sheet;
clouded refuge: regular delight
that multiplies dull humors, gluts the liver,
erects remorse, curl-papers at her temples,
empties the wallet and engenders monsters
(with drooling eyes, gum bones and ill-sealed skull,
a pierced heart that's cured across the Atlantic
after the shame and honor of public collects)
too many tiny coffins rotting in holes,
which must be flowered each November first))
when you can view them, waxen behind glass,
when you can cruise in the safe cove of perfumes,
when you can touch the wrinkle they have in their armpits,
when pleasure bawls from the carrousel's microphone,
when you lick the pink and sepia at their neck
(in the grain of some two-bit photogravure)
when you wander among the intermingling algae,
turning, wild compass whose calm is hard to seize,
black anchor—and they cut the chain, they howl
vainly, so many vessels now swell with blood;
GATHER EACH EVENING there where the former swamp
(up to ramparts where only a watchtower calls

le souvenir) étoile un ciel de nénuphars,
((comme autour d'une viande une escouade de mouches;
autour de la fleur seule émergeant des blés ras,
une dizaine de bourdons, la ruche balayée;
d'un buisson par la chatte amoureuse arrosé,
les frôleurs félins, la moustache électrisée;
de la cloche où se meurt la captive piéride
(un enfant ayant lu Fabre au soir s'en amuse)
l'essaim de papillons que le verre ne leurre;
d'une flûte ambulante et vers le fleuve mue,
les gros rats de harlem et les petits garçons))
et butent d'une rive à l'autre de la rue:
étourneaux dans le ciel (tel l'ouragan déploie
sa noire écharpe à l'heure où le jour se prolonge)
bousculant les passants, arrêtant les voitures,
criant des mots où traine une ordure éventée,
(sans voir le haussement d'épaule des témoins,
sans entendre l'écho de leur voix sur les murs
ouverts où prestement le père encore sévère
repousse dans le noir des cuisines l'enfant)
ou, posant leur divagatoire agitation
en statue de cet âge au milieu de l'asphalte,
trônent, princes muets, de silence saisis,
prêts même à se coucher LE LONG DE LA CHAUSSÉE,
à mourir, lourds du milliard de leurs descendants.

to memory) stars a sky with water lilies,
((as, around meat, a squad of flies; around
a lonely flower emerging from level wheat
ten bumblebees, while their hive is being swept;
around a bush an amorous she-cat's peed on
cat-lechers, electricity in their whiskers;
around the glassbell of a dying Pieridae
(a child who's read Fabre amuses himself one evening)
the swarm of butterflies by the glass unfooled;
around the strolling flute moved riverwards
the giant rats and little boys of Hamelin))
and lurch from one bank to the other of the street:
starlings in the sky (as a hurricane unfolds
its ebony scarf at that hour when day lingers)
jostling pedestrians, stopping automobiles,
yelling cuss-words whose sting has long gone flat
(oblivious of the witnesses' shrugged shoulders
and the echo of their own voices against the walls
open where nimbly a father, still severe,
pushes his child back into the dark kitchen)
or, laying aside their wandering agitation
like modern statues reigning in the center
of the asphalt, dumb princes, by silence overtaken,
ready even to lie down ALONG THE PAVEMENT,
to die, heavy with billions of their descendants.

Arbre

Arbre je te mange sans
Savoir si je t'aime et te
Régurgite parmi des éclaboussures

Arbre tatoué nombril bonhomme
Qui date de l'an dernier
Les calebasses sonores

Arbre des langues haut-parleur
Qui crie avec ses chaussures
Une immobile vérité

Arbre à cloches désolé
Enfant modelé de taches
Et qui pourtant se transforme

Arbre les cheveux déchus
Selon la révulsion des roches
Troupeau de pensées. Fontaine.

Arbre couché sur les lanternes
Champignon du monde printemps
O mon sommeil appétissant.

Tree

Tree I eat you not knowing
If I like you and regurgitate
You amid the splatters

Tattooed tree bellybutton stick figure
That dates from last year
The sonorous bottle-gourds

Tree of tongues loudspeaker
That cries with its shoes
An immobile truth

Desolate tree of bells
Model child modeled with spots
And that changes nevertheless

Tree whose hair is fallen
According to the rocks' revulsion
Flock of ideas. Fountain.

Tree lying on the lanterns
Mushroom, world champion, spring,
O my appetizing sleep.

Perspective

Où je te cherchais ton visage n'existait pas.
Je tenais des mains de confiance ou de sympathie
Mais tu cachais les yeux les clés de ton âme.
J'ai besoin des mots que tu ne dis pas
Des silences des sommeils des peines entre nous deux
Je voudrais t'accompagner jusqu'à tes derniers pas
Même si nous avions à traîner notre vie
Pendant des années d'impatiences de luttes
Je voulais t'aimer mais tu ne t'en doutais pas.
Alors j'ai bu ma solitude j'en ai fait un poison
Qui ne procure pas les ivresses promises
Et la route où je vais est déserte de toi
À mes temps la vie bat aux rythmes de rencontres
Tendues vers ton ombre au-dessus des villes et des champs
Mais tu n'imagines pas tu n'entends pas
Le vrai désir exhalé dans mes nuits par mes nuits près de toi.

Perspective

Where I looked for you your face didn't exist.
I held out hands of trust or sympathy
But you hid your eyes the keys to your soul.
I need the words you don't speak
The silence the sleeps the troubles between the two of us
I'd like to go with you as far as your last steps
Even if we had to drag our life
Through years of impatience of struggle
I wanted to love you but you didn't suspect it.
So I drank my solitude and made a poison of it
That doesn't bring the promised intoxication
And the route I take is bare of you
At my temples life beats to the rhythm of encounters
Stretched toward your shadow above cities and fields
But you don't imagine you don't hear
The real desire exhaled in my nights by my nights next to you.

Cause commune

Les complices couraient les rues, et sans qu'il soit besoin d'une petite annonce, devant les portes attendaient, déjà armés, déjà arrêtés, déjà condamnés, déjà punis, tous ceux qui voulaient m'accompagner dans la ténèbre.

Il ne fallait pas choisir le plus jeune le plus ouvert le plus dodu le plus ensorcelé chacun allait avoir sa part de mes fautes Ils pénétrèrent dans un corps je fus suivi de cette foule.

Quand je voulus désigner ma victime ils l'avaient déjà encapuchonnée Je n'en pus deviner que la forme et la voix Quand je voulus choisir la lame Ils me donnaient un revolver quand je voulus lâcher la balle mes doigts serraient le cou dans la sac et ils éclatèrent de rire quand on m'appela assassin.

Puis ils continuèrent leur chemin tenant leurs mains au fond de mes poches Puis ils m'embrassèrent tour à tour devant ma porte j'ai la trace de ces bouches sur mon sein Ils ont chanté toute la nuit toute toute l'aube toute la journée sous ma fenêtre sous mes oreilles devant mes yeux dans mon sommeil.

Je suis descendu dans la rue J'ai pris ma place dans leur rang Personne ne m'aura choisi je pénétrai dans un seul corps Je savais qui répéterait mon geste de la veille Je ris de voir quel était mort dont il n'avait jamais vu le visage.

Common Cause

The accomplices ran through the streets, and without it needing to be advertised, they were already waiting before the doors, already armed, already arrested, already condemned, already punished, all those who wanted to accompany me into the shadows.

One didn't have to choose the youngest the most open the plumpest the most bewitched each one was going to have his share of my sins They penetrated a body I was followed by that mob.

When I wanted to point out my victim they had already put a hood over his head I could only make out the shape and the voice When I wanted to choose the blade they handed me a revolver when I wanted to release the bullet my fingers squeezed the neck in the sack and they burst out laughing when I was called murderer.

Then they continued on their way with hands thrust deep in my pockets Then they took turns kissing me in front of my door I have the traces of those mouths on my chest They sang all night all dawn all day under my window before my eyes in my sleep.

I went down into the street I took my place in their queue No one will have chosen me I will penetrate a single body I knew he would repeat my gesture of the night before I laughed to see what it was that was dead whose face he had never seen.

Pygmalion

Le bonheur des autres tient-il en ce marbre? Ciseaux de mes veilles, formes de mon rêve, de ce bloc de nuit j'ai fait une épouse. Elle ne répondrait que si je l'appelle.

Froide consomption, étreinte figée. Je puis si je veux tirer de tes seins, tirer de tes bras, tirer de tes hanches, du souple serpent de tes jambes singulières, de ta bouche ligne, de ton sexe étroit, tout ce que j'ai dû tirer de ma tête.

Rien de plus pourtant que ce désir ample. Je criais "Qu'elle ait au moins le regard mobile!" Elle m'a tenu, elle m'a baisé. Elle est descendue de son piédestal. Elle m'a privé de son premier pas. J'aurais tant voulu qu'elle s'en allât seule. Elle ne tient de moi que sa perfection.

Rien de plus pourtant que ce grain poli ... Si je me souviens du bloc équarri si je me souviens du premier éclat, si je me souviens du jaillissement ...! Ah! Combien limpide et combien à moi elle surgissait de l'éternité, elle avait déjà figure mortelle.

Rien de plus pourtant que ce que je voulais. Rien de moins non plus de ce que je ne voulais ... Déjà se mouvant sans que j'y sois rien elle s'en est allée dans le prochain jardin, elle s'est installée dans une ombre humide. Elle est bien partie, j'ai lâché sa main.

Pygmalion

Is the happiness of others contained in this marble? Chisels of my
night work, shapes of my dream, from this block of night I've made a
wife. She would answer only if I called.

Cold consumption, frozen embrace. I can if I wish draw from your
breasts, draw from your arms, draw from your hips, from the supple
serpent of your amazing legs, from your mouth line, from your narrow
sex, everything that I should have drawn from my head.

Nothing more though than this ample desire. I cried, "At least let her
gaze move!" She held me, she kissed me. She descended from her
pedestal. She deprived me of her first step. I would have so liked for
her to go off alone. She resembles me only in her perfection.

Nothing more though than this polished seed . . . If I remember the
squared-off block if I remember the first chip, if I remember the
spurting...! Ah! How limpid and how much mine, she rose out of
eternity, already her face was mortal.

Yet no more than what I wanted. And nothing less than what I
wanted . . . Already moving without my intervention she went off
into the nearby garden, she assumed her post in damp shade. She
really left, I let go her hand.

Psyché

Tes mains nouées, tes mains, tes yeux. Tout un tableau du soir pour des regards qui roulent. Tout une nuit où les formes vraies transparaissent. Et ces blancheurs du jour que tu laisses mourir.

Les cieux baissés, c'est lui, c'est toi. A portée de tes doigts les pommes, les feuillages, les sourires où boire un sommeil étourdi, les longs gisements immobiles, les trésors, les allées et venues, les efforts, les douceurs ... La crainte d'être en retard sur l'horloge.

Que tu dévoiles enfin les soumises parures. Que tu les fasses voir dans l'éclat d'un flambeau. Souffle, souffle. Déjà tu ne peux suivre qu'en esprit la cadence des tes hanches. Et tu cries, et tu cries, attendant d'être prise.

Puis tu cries le plaisir d'être prise. Mille laits ont coulé sur tes jambes. Mille doigts ont saisi ta poitrine, ta gorge. Mille millions de voix sonnent à tes oreilles. C'est la douce et tiède mort. Fais-moi finir de mourir. Et tu attends le matin qui laisse espérer une autre nuit.

Psyche

Your clasped hands, your hands, your eyes. A whole picture of evening
for rolling glances. A whole night for the true forms to show through.
And the whitenesses of the day you let die.

The overcast skies are him, are you. Within reach of your fingers
the apples, the leaves, the smiles where one drinks a mindless sleep,
the long motionless strata, the treasures, the comings and goings, the
efforts, the kindnesses… The fear of being late by the clock.

May you finally unveil the conquered adornments. May you reveal
them in a flash of torchlight. Blow, blow. Already you can follow
only in your mind the rhythm of your hips. And you cry out, you
cry out, waiting to be taken

Then you cry out the pleasure of being taken. A thousand milks have
flowed along your legs. A thousand fingers have seized your breasts,
your throat. A thousand millions of voices are ringing in your ears.
It's the gentle and warm death. Make me finish dying. And you wait
for morning, that lets one hope for another night.

Le Père-Lachaise

Ici rien ne s'aligne dans l'égalité du néant, les monuments comme les épitaphes affirment des différences, tout disparu se retrouve et ressemble aujourd'hui à ce qu'est pour nous son tombeau.

Le Père-Lachaise n'est pas un reposoir oublié autour d'une église, ni un parking éternel labouré pour des légions de cadavres domestiqués : c'est un organisme où la mort transcendée reste vivante, où elle accueille sans agresser.

Les vieillards y regardent approcher leur éternité et elle leur plaît ; les adolescents écoutent monter en eux la sève qui passera un jour sous ces dalles, et ils s'en foutent ; les bébés s'enivrent de l'odeur des thuyas tandis que leur mère murmure la musique gravée sur un socle de statue.

À peine poussée la porte d'une chapelle mal fermée, un cercueil crevé expose sans éveiller l'horreur curieuse des passants, des ossements bousculés par le rase-mottes d'un ange.

Sous un auvent, depuis cent ans, une photographie émaillée reflète d'inextinguibles clins d'oeil. Un buste que l'on caresse sous un dolmen établit la communication avec les puissances souterraines ; un gisant que l'on chevauche procure des envolées vers l'extase. Mainte allégorie, maint symbole égaré nourrissent l'évasive rêverie.

Le poids des pierres descellées impose un air penché au tronc des noyers noirs d'Amérique. Les primevères de zinc, les roses de polystyrène, les chrysanthèmes de céramique épousent le lierre rampant entre les buis bien engraissés. La grille de bronze supporte des racines aériennes : le sol trop encombré refuse parfois le végétal.

Les génies morts trop tôt ou trop tard coudoient les familles ignorées.

Père-Lachaise

Here, nothing is lined up in the equality of nothingness; both monuments and epitaphs affirm differences; each of the departed is found again and resembles today what his tomb is for us.

Père-Lachaise is not a forgotten station in a procession around a church nor an eternal parking lot ploughed for legions of domesticated corpses; it is an organism where death, transcended, is still alive and welcomes you without provocation.

Here, old people look at their eternity coming closer and they like it; adolescents listen to the sap rising in them which shall one day flower under these flagstones and don't give a damn; babies are drunk with the scent of thuyas while their mothers hum the music engraved on the pedestals of statues.

As soon as you push the rickety door of a chapel a small coffin reveals, without arousing the inquisitive horror of passersby, bones that have just been jostled by a hedgehopping angel.

Under a wooden canopy, an enameled photograph has been winking for the last hundred hears. You rub a bust under a dolmen and establish communication with subterranean powers. You straddle a recumbent figure on a tomb and take off toward ecstasy. Many allegories, many misplaced symbols nourish evasive daydreams.

The slanted gravestones lean their weight against the trunks of the American black-walnut trees. Zinc primroses, polyester roses, and ceramic chrysanthemums mingle with creeping ivy among the well-fertilized boxwood trees. Aerial roots are propped up by bronze fence posts. The overcrowded ground sometimes refuses what is vegetal.

Geniuses who died too soon or too late rub elbows with obscure

Les idoles de tous les cultes se mêlent au Bottin de siècles révolus comme on bat des cartes en se figurant d'autres jeux. Un nom suffit à ne dire rien à personne. Un autre à provoquer des transes. Un autre accroche les éclaboussures de passions jamais assouvies.

Rien n'est rien. L'or de syllabes fanées allume le poli des granits. Un bloc de marbre noir prend vie sous l'escargot qui l'escalade. Un vitrail ouvre le ciel entre des stalactites de larme.

Ici les coeurs éteints perpétuent leur rumeur dans la promiscuité de palpitations neuves. Le vertical s'enfonce un peu plus vite dans le temps, c'est tout. L'allongé a pour lui la patience.

Tout autour des murs le monde court à sa fatale fin. Un jour, miroir renversé, la ville entière sera ce cimetière seul debout parmi ses ombres, avec le souvenir de toute notre vie.

families. The idols of all the cults are jumbled with the social registers of vanished centuries as one shuffles cards for one game while thinking of another. One name is enough to mean nothing to anyone. Another to induce trances. Another is splattered with passions which will never be slaked.

Nothing is nothing. The gold of faded syllables lights up the granite's polished surface. A block of black marble comes to life under the snail that is climbing it. A stained-glass window opens up the sky between stalactites of tears.

Here burnt-out hearts perpetuate their throbbing in the nearness of new palpitations. The vertical man sinks a little more quickly into time, that's all. The horizontal one has patience on his side.

All around the walls the world hastens towards its fatal end. One day, the whole city will be reversed in the mirror of this cemetery, which will stand alone with its shadows, with the memory of all our lives.

Quel enfant?

Il fallut longtemps pour trouver un nom à cet enfant,
Assis sur une marche devant le seuil
Il cachait son visage dans ses mains
Ou bien voilait ses yeux de ses cheveux
Lorsque le vent sur son dos froissait ses ailes.
Longtemps nous ne l'avons même pas distingué
Tant nous habitait la chaleur de notre âge
Nous n'entendions pas ses soupirs ni ses chants
Les prenant pour la rumeur de notre sang
Nous l'avons roulé comme un galet sur le sable
C'était le temps où nous ne pensions pas au temps
Où nous ne savions pas regarder notre image
Dans l'image de nous que nous renvoyait l'autre
Où nous ne voyons pas cet enfant sur le seuil.

What Child?

It took a long time to find a name for that child.
Sitting on a step in front of the threshold
He hid his face in his hands
Or veiled his eyes with his hair
When the wind at his back bruised his wings.
For a long time we didn't even notice him,
So deeply did the heat of our age inhabit us
We heard neither his sighs nor his songs
Mistaking them for the murmur of our blood
We rolled him along the sand like a pebble
It was the time when we didn't think of time
When we didn't know how to look at our image
In the image the other reflected back
When we didn't see that child on the threshold.

Complainte de l'amant

Mon amant mon amant fait durer le temps
Avec la toison de nos désirs
Nous tricotons un bonheur chaud

Mon amant mon amant fait durer la nuit
Que cette lampe demeure
Le symbole ardent de nos joies

Nous brûlons et nous éclairons
Et nous mourons
Lumière chaleur avec la nuit.

Avant qu'il ne ferme la porte
Y laisserai-je tous nos doigts?
Quand il aura fermé la porte
Serai-je amputée des deux mains?

Mon amant mon amant fait durer l'agonie
Je ne serai jamais qu'un coeur
Pourras-tu le rendre éternel?

Quand il versera du vinaigre
Sur le marbre sépulchral
Le marbre se désagrégera
Et souffrirai—je sans mourir?

Il ne reste de moi debout
Qu'une carcasse en fil de fer
Où pend interminablement
Le sexe séché d'un amant.

The Lover's Complaint

My lover my lover makes time last
With the fleece of our desires
We knit a warm happiness

My lover my lover makes the night last
May this lamp remain
The eager symbol of our delight

We burn and we give off light
And we die,
Heat, light with the night.

Before he shuts the door
Will all our fingers get caught?
Once he has closed the door
Will my two hands be cut off?

My lover my lover makes the death agony last
I'll never be anything but a heart
Can you somehow make it eternal?

When he pours the vinegar
On the sepulchral marble
Will the marble break up
And will I suffer without dying?

Of me standing, there remains
Nothing but a wire carcass
On which hangs, interminably,
The dried sex of a lover.

Appendix I: Translation
with Lost French Original

Bridge Passed

The bridge once passed
My city shows its wrinkles
Deep furrows always empty streets
Dead shops drawn shutters
It's the face it used to have
In the days when witches died
When from slow boats Negroes
In red shirts disembarked
To dissolve in the nights
And impregnated the young virgins
And made the boys dream
Of impossible adventures
It's the face it put on
In July nineteen forty
When young half-naked Aryans
Machine guns at their shoulders
Intoned the Horst Wessel song
And struck echoes from the walls
Of the never-violated city
Memories lived or learned
Flow together this Sunday
Like the waters of the two rivers
And evening descends slowly
Until night along the embankment
Lights a few streetlamps
Whose reflection at the base of the bridge
Inducted me as a child
Into impossible dreaming

Flow together this Sunday

From *A Public Space*, no. 5 (2008)

Appendix II: Poem Written in French
and English

From *Locus Solus*, nos. 3-4 (1961)

Tchat

YES-YES-YES-YES-YES

                    YES   YES   YES

Esteban   sensible   band   blues
   telefon   immédiate   and   bou
              ment   bu
                                                      bu
   Thèbesphinx   terrible
                    say   Toù

No No Sing Sin et m'a péché moi
      ronto
A l'op   mouchi mouchi   noix
      éra
         Turandot she knows about août en doux

j'étais là l'amant longtemps   ago
   Nature   apporte   odor épure   oho!
Blanche main rturn   regard   trois
   Marines   of course trois soleils
                         suns   Maman Lou
                         sons

Garanty jardin massacré marque
                    parceque beaux
Bel angel général   perle françois
Orchestra toi ma pieuvre ma reine ma pluie
Liebelei bl huitre riche os tree
Vasustrade bal et lit lee
Black hand   retour look   three
   Marines of course   3 fois
                    times   OUI

245

Appendix III: Variant French and English Texts

Translator's Note: These two translations differ somewhat from the French texts printed here. The versions I translated have apparently been lost.

L'Heure de musique

L'Heure de musique

Une femme se penche hors des silences de l'ennui
Une femme s'ouvre le corsage pour y lire des notes
Car les sons ressemblent à ceux qui n'ont pas lu tous les visages
Cueillis au hasard qui marquent la vie pour une page entière.
Les sons se plient en feuilles qui épousent les coupoles
En de grands battements ordonnés par le vent selon le rite.
Les sons se fardent de couleurs atroces
Couleur de sang séché de la couleur
De sang sec qu'aura le nôtre
Et ils demeurent à peine pour passer
De l'état d'une vibration à celui d'une autre
Du rouge au noir mat
Du liquide au solide
De debout à couché
D'être à pourrir.
Les sons s'allongent en guirlandes de riens
Ce n'est qu'air lancé en l'air qui vient heurter
La pellicule de chair bien irriguée
Et nous posons la main sur notre coeur
En formulant des abstractions biologiques.
Les sons sont une ronde d'enfançons
Qui tournent joyeux à la façon
Des grands gyroscopes cosmiques
Dans le sens des aiguilles d'une montre
Dans le sens au moins du Soleil
Si les étoiles sont sans importance . . .

Mais que les amitiés les groupent en cercle fermé
En anneau pour les fastes d'une noce

The Hour of Music

A woman leans out of the silences of boredom
A woman opens her blouse to read notes there
For the sounds resemble those passages in the Bible
Gleaned by chance that mark life for a whole page
Unrecognizable to him who hasn't already seen all the faces;
The sounds fold into leaves whose shapes fit the cupolas
With a great flapping that the wind directs according to the rite;
The sounds paint their faces horrible colors
Color of dried blood of the color
Of the dry blood that ours will be
And they barely stay in order to pass
From the state of one vibration to that of another
From red to matte black
From liquid to solid
From standing to lying down
From being to rotting
The sounds stretch out into garlands of nothing
It's nothing but air that stirs without cadence without rhythm
It's nothing but air tossed in the air that comes up against
The film of well-irrigated flesh
That taut membrane on a drum of resonances;
And we place our hands on our hearts
To formulate biological abstractions;
The sounds are children dancing in a round
Spinning on a point
Like the great cosmic gyroscopes
In the direction of the hands of a watch
In the direction of a sun at least
If the direction of the stars is without importance . . .

But that the friendships group them in closed circles
In rings to celebrate a wedding

Alors les nuits s'abreuvent à des calices renversés
Comme un essaim d'abeilles autour d'une reine neuve
Un réseau de lumière écrase les secrets d'une allée
Rideaux flacons agités parfums
Que la narine retrouve avec reconnaissance
Des chairs des regards des étreintes.
Car le corps est aussi de gammes et d'harmonies
Et l'âme se laisse aller au plus haut
Comme une chemise hélant au secours lors d'un naufrage
L'âme reste à ne rien demander qu'un secours
Se tait candide au-delà de tout geste
Se résout en une horizontale chute sans fin
Entre deux pesanteurs rivales qui s'annulent
Elle est seule hors des nuits que laisse le Soleil sur la Terre
Il n'y a pas de nuit sans qu'il n'y ait de Soleil
Il n'y a pas de musique sans moi.

Then the nights drink from the inverted chalice
Like a swarm of bees around a new queen
A network of light crushes the secrets of a walkway,
Curtains, shaken flasks, perfumes
The nostril finds again with gratitude,
Flesh, glances, hugs . . .
For the body is also scales and harmonies
And the soul lets itself go only higher
Like a shirt calling for help from a shipwreck,
The soul stays asking nothing but help,
Keeps its peace frank beyond all gestures,
Resolves itself into an endless horizontal fall
Between two rival, equal weights;
It is alone outside the nights the sun makes on earth
There are no nights without sun
There is no earth without me.

Listen
  don't keep anything of the noise outside
  except this phrase
  that descends
    the steps
      of a house
        in silence
The sounds of your heart make a storm on the beach
The restlessness of your nerves makes a hurricane on a forest
The movements of your lips ransack the flowerbeds
Buried under green precautions
And that it was necessary to try to reach, only
      through motionlessness
      through patience
      through prudence
      through velvet
      through honey

A reed signal
A shudder of catgut
A pipe of agile tongues

An arch of reverie
A porch of lies
A roof that doesn't shelter one from anything

A joy of looking
A joy of not seeing

A joy of hearing dying
Along along the deserted avenues
The steps and the steps of those who regret their steps

It's the daily hour of inaccessible
Musics

HERE   stretches out
    I   extends
And if the bandstand on the mall
Is empty
Here I populate the expanse
Here I populate the immense sphere
            of everything that isn't
                    me
Of everything that is me
            of everything that isn't just
                    me
Of everything that is also other
Of everything I become
Of everything I am
Of everything I'm not
Of everything I want
Of everything that is me

Of everything that isn't just me
Of everything I ask
Of nothing

Of nothing that mills the weather
And the weather is nothing to me

Of nothing that tears space
And I measure up to the least standard

Of nothing that distills my life
And my life is my life

Of nothing I lose
and have nothing to gain

Of nothing I ask for
And I have everything

It's the daily hour of musics
You dispense
At the edge of the world
For a single ear
Folded back like a shell
Wherein rolls the sound of former seas
Round like the world
And like me
Closed like the world
Open on the worlds
Placed near the dark center
Near that potential volcano
Those sleepy monsters
For a long time
For such a long time long time

That you mistake them for georgic hills
That you mistake them for the tombs of legendary kings
That you lie down there
That you like it there
That you slaughter each other there
Indolently
But with composure
As though there were nothing there that could react
Nothing lay there that could see or think
Nothing but an old skeleton adorned with rusty armor
A dust of man that isn't even proud
Of its descent from the great monkeys . . .
Here I exhaust my substance in useless ardors
The cold the shadows the dank prisons
Have merely polished me a bit better each day
And on all my surfaces
As long as I am blade of bone become
Transparent filter through which all realities pass.
I have none left, but they pass,
But they lose
                        I have none left
                        a heap of by-products
                        a slag hummock
But they keep the worst of themselves
The power to touch me pass through me
Move me

And you can let them escape now
For the round the flight you meant for them
The harm is done it is indeed done
Now they've become inoffensive doves.

From *o•blek* 7 (Spring 1990)

Calendrier

Calendrier

Je suis rentré, nous avons fait les comptes
Assis devant le pain:
Le fils mort-né, les pommes de l'autre année,
Tout ce que coûta notre vie.

Nous avons oublié la promenade aux bagues
Jetées un soir dans la Seine parce que
L'eau appelle l'anneau
Et la robe achetée trop étroite exprès
Que nous devions revêtir ensemble.

A voir les chiffres noirs sur blanc les larmes
Nous ont glissé sous les doigts.
Tandis que chante le tonnerre
Un train dépasse un train
Vers la Bretagne d'où nous sommes venus hier
Le musoir aux vagues usées
Les goélands fumant devant le soleil rouge
Les bateaux rapportaient des médailles
Légendes toujours mal finies
Il y avait un merle en cage
Cadeau d'un oncle célibataire
Dont nous gardions la photographie
Dans un bocal de confitures.

Calendar

I came home, we made out the accounts
Sitting in front of the bread:
The stillborn son, the apples of last year,
All that our life had cost us.
We forgot the walk with the rings
Thrown one evening into the Seine because
Water attracts rings
And the dress bought too tight on purpose
That we could put on together.

At the sight of the black figures on white the tears
Slipped between our fingers.
While the water boils a whistle announces
A train passing a train
Toward Brittany from which we came once upon a time
The waves wore away the steps of the pier
The gulls smoking in front of the red sun
The boats brought back medals
Legends that never ended right

There was a blackbird in a cage
A present from a bachelor uncle
Whose photograph we kept
In a jar of jam
For greedy collations
When the wet seasons return
And the pirate's sword
Out of its sheath bloody point
To impregnate sick fairies

On the kitchen tile a faded child
Kneeling in prayer the curled wheat the wind

In the curtains to go away alone
You were sleeping naked stitched with silence
Pale clock the afternoon
Ready for the yeast weaving your basket
Hair stretched tight between your teeth
Attentive to the expected music
To the waves rolling future reminiscences

Dulled pride glues us to the bed
The rivers cover the palms
A printed shroud teaches us the phrases
Of the evening the monochrome dreams the refusals
The lamp burns lower and the swallows listen
In the dull sound of dusty furniture
To our death falling face to face like a window
Between two walls where the shadow harnesses its horses
The price of mourning is posted under our eyelids.

From *A Public Space*, no. 5 (2008)

Appendix IV: Bibliography

Periodical and Anthology Publications for Ashbery Translations of Martory Poems

"Ballad." *Mantis* 2 (2001), pp. 195–196.

"Bastille." *Poetry*, vol. 177, no. 1 (Oct.–Nov. 2000), p. 18.

"Before, During, After." *To* (Summer 1992), p. 15.

"Black Diamond." *The New Yorker* (June 10, 1991), p. 46.

"Blues." *The KGB Bar Book of Poems*, ed. David Lehman and Star Black (New York: Perennial/Harper Collins, 2000), pp. 133–134.

"Bridge Passed." *A Public Space,* no. 5 (2008).

"Broken Solitude." *o•blek* 8 (Fall 1990), p. 63.

"The Buying Back." *Conjunctions*, no. 38 (2002), pp. 328–329.

"The Cage." *To* (Summer 1992), p. 16.

"Calendar." *A Public Space,* no. 5 (2008).

"Career." *o•blek* 5 (Spring 1989), p. 26.

"Chocolate Poem." *Lingo* (Spring/Summer 1993), p. 68.

"Coming and Going." *Poetry*, vol. 162, no. 3 (June 1993), p. 133.

"Common Cause." *Conjunctions*, no. 38 (2002), p. 330.

"The Crossroads." Thomas Breidenbach and Pierre Martory, *Poems*

([New York]: November 11, 1996), pamphlet, n. p.; *Verse*, vol. 13, no. 1 (1996), p. 65.

"Early Morning." *Conjunctions*, no. 38 (2002), p. 328.

"Elegy." *Poetry*, vol. 162, no. 3 (June 1993), p. 135.

"Evenings in Rochefort." *Locus Solus*, nos. 3–4 (1961), pp. 122–131.

"From a Private Domain." *Trafika* 5 (Autumn 1995), p. 166.

"Ganymede." *o•blek* 8 (Fall 1990), pp. 59–62.

"The Hour of Music." *o•blek* 7 (Spring 1990), pp. 84–88.

"The Landscape Is behind the Door." Translated by John Ashbery. Introduction to poem by Dara Wier. In *Dark Horses: Poets on Overlooked Poems*. Edited by Joy Katz and Kevin Prufer. Urbana: University of Illinois Press, 2007.

"Litanies." *Conjunctions*, no. 38 (2002), pp. 331–332.

"The Main Thing in a Face Can Be Read on a Freezing Day." *Conjunctions*, no. 38 (2002), p. 331.

"Music." *Conjunctions*, no. 38 (2002), p. 332–334.

"Nothing to Say." *The World* 46 (Feb. 1993), p. 75.

"Obscure Gestures." *Trafika* 5 (Autumn 1995), p. 165.

"Oh, Lake . . . ." *Trafika* 5 (Autumn 1995), p. 168.

"Passing the Frontier." *Poetry*, vol. 162, no. 3 (June 1993), p. 132.

"Perspective." *Mantis* 2 (2001), pp. 196–197.

"Red and Black Lake." *The World* 46 (Feb. 1993), pp. 74–75.

"Scintillating Sky." Thomas Breidenbach and Pierre Martory, *Poems* ([New York]: November 11, 1996), pamphlet, n. p.; *Verse*, vol. 13, no. 1 (1996), p. 64.

"Serenity." *Mantis* 2 (2001), pp. 198–199.

"Soirée." *o•blek* 8 (Fall 1990), p. 58.

"Tchat." *Locus Solus*, nos. 3–4 (1961), pp. 132–133.

"Ten Years for Example After." *Trafika* 5 (Autumn 1995), p. 169.

"Town Hall, Fifteenth Arrondissement." *Poetry*, vol. 177, no. 1 (Oct.–Nov. 2000), p. 17.

"Tree." Thomas Breidenbach and Pierre Martory, *Poems* ([New York]: November 11, 1996), pamphlet, n. p.; *Verse*, vol. 13, no. 1 (1996), p. 66.

"Undecipherable Archives." *Lingo* (Spring/Summer 1993), p. 67.

"Unnatural History." *Conjunctions*, no. 38 (2002), pp. 329–330.

"A Visit." *o•blek* 5 (Spring 1989), pp. 27–28.

"Without Rhyme or Reason." *Trafika* 5 (Autumn 1995), p. 167.

"Wine." *Poetry*, vol. 162, no. 3 (June 1993), p. 134.

Previously Unpublished Translations

Calm Water
Collusion
The Lover's Complaint
Pygmalion
Psyche
What Child?

Poetry Books and Other Publications by Pierre Martory

Every Question but One. Translated by John Ashbery. New York: Intuflo Editions, The Groundwater Press, 1990.

The Landscape Is behind the Door. Translated by John Ashbery. New York: Sheep Meadow Press, 1994.

Oh, lac/Oh, Lake. With monotypes by Francis Wishart. Edited by Olivier Brossard and Eugene Richie. Hove, East Sussex, England: Artery Editions, 2008.

"Le Père-Lachaise" / "Père-Lachaise." French text for Francis Wishart's suite of etchings, *Le Père-Lachaise.* Translation by John Ashbery published as companion piece to French edition for first American exhibition of the etchings, Gotham Book Mart, 1979. Printed by Leonard Seastone. New York: Tideline Press, 1979.

Poems. Thomas Breidenbach and Pierre Martory. Pamplet. New York: November 11, 1996.

Veilleur de jours. New York and Paris: Alyscamps Press–Sheep Meadow Press, 1997.

Notes on the Editors

Eugene Richie

Eugene Richie edited John Ashbery's *Selected Prose* and coedited with Olivier Brossard *Oh, lac / Oh, Lake* (Artery Editions, 2008)—a bilingual volume of Pierre Martory's poems, translated by Ashbery. His poetry collections include *Island Light* (Painted Leaf Press, 1998) and *Place du Carousel* (Zilvinas and Daiva Publications, 2001) with Rosanne Wasserman, with whom he founded The Groundwater Press. With Edith Grossman, he co-translated Jaime Manrique's poetry books *Scarecrow* (The Groundwater Press, 1990) and *My Night with Federico García Lorca* (Painted Leaf Press, 1997; University of Wisconsin Press, 2003). He teaches at Pace University in New York City, where he is also the Director of Writing.

Rosanne Wasserman

Rosanne Wasserman edited John Ashbery's Charles Eliot Norton Lectures, *Other Traditions*, and assisted with the editing of Ashbery's *Selected Prose*. Her poems have appeared widely in journals and anthologies, including twice in *Best American Poetry* (Macmillan, 1988 and 1994), chosen by John Ashbery and A. R. Ammons. Her poetry books include *The Lacemakers* and *No Archive on Earth* (Gnosis Press, 1992, 1995); *Other Selves* (Painted Leaf Press, 1999); and *Place du Carousel* (Zilvinas and Daiva Publications, 2001), with Eugene Richie. Together, they direct the Groundwater Press, a non-profit poetry publisher. She teaches in the Humanities Department of the United States Merchant Marine Academy, Kings Point, New York.